WEDDING ETIQUETTE
PROPERLY EXPLAINED

Where to find *Right Way*

Elliot *Right Way* take pride in our editorial quality, accuracy and value-for-money. Booksellers everywhere can rapidly obtain any *Right Way* book for you. If you have been particularly pleased with any one title, do please mention this to your bookseller as personal recommendation helps us enormously.

Please send to the address on the back of the title page opposite, a stamped, self-addressed envelope if you would like a copy of our *free catalogue*. Alternatively, you may wish to browse through our extensive range of informative titles arranged by subject on the Internet at **www.right-way.co.uk**

We welcome views and suggestions from readers as well as from prospective authors; do please write to us or e-mail:
info@right-way.co.uk

WEDDING ETIQUETTE

PROPERLY EXPLAINED

Marriage under all Denominations and Civil Ceremonies

Vernon Heaton

RIGHT WAY

Typeset in 10½pt Times by Letterpart Limited, Reigate, Surrey.

Printed and bound in Great Britain by Cox & Wyman Ltd., Reading, Berkshire.

The *Right Way* series is published by Elliot Right Way Books, Brighton Road, Lower Kingswood, Tadworth, Surrey, KT20 6TD, U.K. For information about our company and the other books we publish, visit our website at www.right-way.co.uk

CONTENTS

INTRODUCTION

The vast majority of the population take the marriage vows at least once during their lifetime.

The profusion of wedding magazines and the delight with which stories of celebrity weddings are lapped up testify to the endurance of the idea of a wedding as the ultimate romantic adventure.

Yet in the midst of that romantic dream there are essential legal obligations to be fulfilled. There are also many customs that could be observed, perhaps only half remembered yet often considered vital to the success of the day!

This book is therefore designed to meet the needs of those who wish to know and follow the exact details of the formalities and the long-established customs expected of a wedding – and to give an insight into the legal requirements that must be met before a marriage can take place.

1

CAN YOU MARRY
A RELATION?
THE LEGAL POINTS

Certain marriages are prohibited where the couple are held to be too closely related. The Book of Common Prayer lists the forbidden marriages as follows:

A man may not marry his
  mother, daughter, father's mother, mother's mother, son's daughter, daughter's daughter, sister, father's daughter, mother's daughter, wife's mother, wife's daughter, father's wife, son's wife, father's father's wife, mother's father's wife, wife's father's mother, wife's mother's mother, wife's son's daughter, wife's daughter's daughter, son's son's wife, daughter's son's wife, father's sister, mother's sister, brother's daughter or sister's daughter.

A woman may not marry her
  father, son, father's father, mother's father, son's son, brother, father's son, mother's son, husband's father, husband's son, mother's husband, daughter's husband, father's mother's husband, mother's mother's husband, husband's father's father, husband's mother's father, husband's son's son, husband's daughter's son, son's daughter's husband, daughter's daughter's husband, father's brother, mother's brother, brother's son or sister's son.

The terms 'brother' and 'sister' include half-blood relationships.

The Marriage (Enabling) Act (England, Scotland & Wales) and the Matrimonial Causes (Northern Ireland) Order 1978 followed on from earlier Acts and permit a man's marriage to his deceased wife's sister, aunt or niece, deceased brother's or uncle's or nephew's widow, deceased wife's brother's daughter, deceased wife's sister's daughter, father's deceased brother's widow, mother's deceased brother's widow, deceased wife's father's sister, deceased wife's mother's sister, brother's deceased son's widow and sister's deceased son's widow.

The Marriage (Prohibited Degrees of Relationship) Act 1986 (for England, Scotland and Wales, but not Northern Ireland) allows a man to marry his mother-in-law, step-daughter, step-mother, or daughter-in-law without having to obtain a private Act of Parliament. The Act also allows a woman to marry her father-in-law, step-son, step-father, or son-in-law. However, there are certain other conditions which have to be met before the marriages can take place; in particular, for marriages between in-laws, the respective former spouses will have to have died. Marriages under this Act can take place by Licence or by a Superintendent Registrar's Certificate. They may take place in the Church of England, though not after the publication of banns.

A clergyman who may have scruples over solemnising a marriage where the degree of relationship – though now legal – is, or may have been, traditionally proscribed by ecclesiastical law, is entitled to refuse to do so, though he may, if he so wishes, allow another clergyman to use his church for the purpose. A superintendent registrar, however, must marry a couple so long as they are legally free to marry.

If either party has been married previously, he or she must produce to the superintendent registrar documentary proof of their legal ability to re-marry. Where the original partner has died, a death certificate is necessary to establish that proof, and where he or she has been divorced, the decree absolute is required. A decree *nisi* is not enough in England and Wales. (In Scotland a divorce becomes absolute as soon as it is granted.)

In England and Wales both parties to a marriage must have reached the age of 16; under the age of 18 the couple will need the consent of their parents, or guardians. Such permission must be given in writing and signed by both the minor's parents or guardians.

Where the parents or guardians are abroad their signature to the letter of consent needs to be properly witnessed, usually by a notary public or perhaps a consul.

Where there is neither a parent nor a guardian, a minor has the right to apply to the courts for permission to marry and, similarly, where he or she feels that a parent's or guardian's permission is being unreasonably refused, an application to overrule their decision can be made to the same court.

In Scotland, any two persons may marry, regardless of where they live, provided that they are both 16 years of age on the day of their marriage, that they are unmarried, that they are not related to one another in a forbidden degree, that they are not of the same sex, that they are capable of understanding the nature of a marriage ceremony and of consenting to marriage, and that the marriage would be regarded as valid in any foreign country to which either party belongs.

In all cases there must be at least two witnesses to the marriage who must be over 18 years of age (16 in Scotland). The clergyman and/or the registrar cannot act as a witness to the marriage.

2

ENGAGEMENT DETAILS

Whereas once the parent's consent would be sought before a proposal was formally put, nowadays the first they may know of it is the flash of a sparkling new ring. However, they are still entitled to some courtesy and as the odds are that they may well be paying for the wedding and reception (or meeting a considerable part of the cost) it is only right that they be informed of the decision as soon as possible.

The bride's parents should be the first to be told. (Consent would, of course, be necessary if the girl is under age.) Then follows the man's parents – and thereafter the announcement may be broadcast as widely as the couple wish.

The formality of an announcement in the press is much more rare than it used to be; most people are told as and when the couple happen to meet them. But if the announcement is made through the newspapers, it is proper to inform relatives and close friends verbally in advance. (See Chapters 11 and 12 for the wording of announcements and invitations, etc.)

The next consideration is the engagement ring, which is thought to set the seal on the betrothal of the pair and is in itself a warning to other men not to poach. Whilst the most romantic dreams often have the proposal being made by the proffering of a sparkling ring in a neat square box, many would-be grooms err on the side of caution and allow their fiancées to select a ring once the proposal has been accepted.

Though an engagement ring is still the prized possession of most girls who have 'found their man' – and remains the prized token of those who have subsequently married – its intrinsic value is perhaps less of an assurance of the man's depth of feeling today, than of the common sense of the pair who have taken into careful consideration their financial situation, prospects and intentions.

A sensible couple will have set a budget before they go shopping, bearing in mind other expenses such as a down-payment on a house or the quantity and quality of furniture, etc., that they will wish to purchase and the likely cost of any loan/hire purchase commitments they may soon be making. But however intrinsically valueless the ring, its symbolic superstition makes it almost a 'must'.

Instead of the more usual diamonds, it is common for a couple to economise by selecting a cheaper stone. Cubic zirconia or man-made diamonds are increasingly popular, and birthstones come and go in popularity with current fashion.

Birthstones are generally accepted as being for the

January girl	**Garnets**	meaning	*Constancy*
February	**Amethysts**		*Sincerity*
March	**Bloodstones**		*Courage*
April	**Diamonds**		*Purity*
May	**Emeralds**		*Hope*
June	**Pearls** or **Agates**		*Health*
July	**Rubies**		*Passion*
August	**Sardonyx**		*Married happiness*
September	**Sapphires**		*Repentance*
October	**Topaz**		*A lovable nature*
November	**Opals**		*Cheerfulness*
December	**Turquoise** or **Lapis Lazuli**		*Unselfishness*

The majority of wedding rings sold are nine carat gold and when buying the engagement ring it is just as well to consider this as most brides like their rings to be the same colour! (The nine carat rings will stand up to the friction of two rubbing together better than a higher carat.) There is also a choice of white gold or platinum. In the past a plain gold band was most common but now there is a wide range of patterned rings to choose from.

In return for the engagement ring, it is usual for the girl to give her betrothed an engagement present – again, of course, limited in value to the means at her disposal after more practical matters have been considered. A gold chain or tie clip or some piece of jewellery such as a signet ring are the more usual gifts for such an occasion.

Though the engaged couple are expected from now on to be kept very busy with the arrangements for their future – the wedding itself, the reception afterwards, the honeymoon, their new home and the furniture that is needed for it (and even the trivialities of negotiations with the electricity and gas companies and so on . . .) – they still have to give some thought to their social obligations.

The engagement party is the most urgent of these and it usually takes place on the day the announcement is made in the press or shortly afterwards. It is at the party that the official announcement of the engagement is made – if it has not already been published in the press.

It is obvious that the engagement party should be held as soon as possible after the couple have agreed to marry. It would be difficult to maintain the secret for long in any event and the party loses a lot of its glamour if it is staged long after everybody knows the reason for it and all the congratulations and good wishes have been expressed.

Long engagements are often considered unnecessary, but if the wedding is to be conducted with all the trappings, on a day and time convenient to most of the guests, and a reception is to follow, a certain lapse of time is inevitable. Many couples are anxious to marry; all of them seem to prefer much the same date and reception rooms, the same honeymoon hotels and even the same photographer – which means that a good deal of planning is necessary before arrangements can be finalised.

The engagement party is usually a more informal affair and leaves the couple with a wide choice at their disposal. Again, the first consideration must be the cost, though it is quite usual for the bride's parents to pay for it, whatever the scale. However, as the same people are generally expected to have to pay for the wedding reception in due course, it can be quite a strain on them if thought isn't given to the matter from the very beginning.

The party may be held at the home of either set of parents,

though, again, it is more usual to hold it at the bride's home. It is her father who makes the official announcement of the engagement.

It might be confined to a family party of, say, both sets of parents, brothers and sisters – and maybe those grandparents who are able to be there. The numbers can be increased, of course, though a lot of care must be taken in the selection. Aunts are inclined to be upset if they have been left out for a close friend and close friends are likely to be resentful if some long neglected relative is included instead of them. Tact is essential.

Of course the numbers can be expanded *ad infinitum* by hiring a hall, but many prefer to make the occasion as intimate as possible. If larger numbers are to be invited than it is possible to cater for at home, a restaurant may be a better place for the party. Everything is supplied, cooked and served – and even the bride's mother has a chance to enjoy herself.

However, even here the guests should be selected with care. It is quite usual for the young couple and their equally young friends to go on from the dinner party in the restaurant – or even from their home – perhaps to a disco or a night club afterwards. The older generation will not be expected to accompany them, nor should the parents resent being abandoned by the younger element.

The arrangements for the party in a restaurant or a hotel are quite straightforward. The hotelier or the restaurateur will advise you of exactly what you should do to make the occasion a success. He will advise on the menu, the table decorations, the seating, the wines and even on the speeches if the host is at all doubtful about the procedure.

The meal itself need not be too costly, depending, of course, on the menu, the standard of the hotel or restaurant and the style of the service. Wines will add considerably to the bill if a lot of discretion is not used. Nor is it necessary to have wines – perhaps just a sherry or port with the speeches and always, of course, fruit juice or other soft drinks. (For those who might like to spread their wings on the party there are a few suggestions for menus in Chapter 19.)

The couple will, of course, be given the place of honour at the table and if the party is given at home, they will be excused from the usual chores of serving and washing-up afterwards. The bride-to-be's parents will sit next to her while the future bride-groom's parents will find their places at his side. This will be varied at the wedding reception after they are married, where the bride will sit on her groom's left side as tradition dictates.

The only speeches that are required are two. The first will be made by the girl's father when he either announces the engagement of his daughter or wishes them both health and happiness. The future son-in-law replies on behalf of himself and his fiancée in proposing the health of their parents. The speeches are usually light-hearted as it is a happy occasion and other toasts may be drunk if the mood of the party permits.

If the younger people are to go on elsewhere or are to dance at the hotel where the engagement party has been given, a move should be made immediately after the speeches – either by the couple who will lead their friends away, or by the parents who will leave their children to their own devices, depending on whether the further entertainment is to be held there or elsewhere.

As the party is informal, dress is usually lounge suits for the men and semi-evening wear for the women. Printed invitations are unusual (unless the party is to be wide in scope) and even hand-written invitations are the exception, a telephone call being the usual thing.

Place-cards and a table plan are considered unnecessary too. Everybody knows that the engaged couple will occupy the seats of honour and that their parents will sit on either side of them. After that, the girl's father, as the host, will suggest where his guests should sit as they come to the table.

Of course, a wise host will know his guests in advance – or find out about those he does not know. This enables him to know who should sit next to whom; it could be pretty disastrous to sit old enemies next to one another! But he should still pay regard to the custom that the sexes should alternate.

Sometimes it happens that the girl and her betrothed come from far apart; maybe the man is a Londoner and his wife-to-be an Edinburgh girl. Obviously it is impossible to bring everybody who has to be at the party all the way from London, but as the hosts are the parents of the bride-to-be, the venue will almost certainly be in Scotland. In such an event the girl should try and make it possible to attend a similar party in London. This party will be entirely informal, usually at the man's home or that of his parents, and limited to those who were unable to travel north for the official party. If this is not practicable, the couple should try to bring the two sets of parents together wherever it can be arranged. At that gathering there will be no need to invite anyone else – with the possible exception of brothers, sisters and grand-parents.

An engagement is a much less formal affair than it was in years gone by. It is still a contract, of course, though not in itself unbreakable without recourse to law. However, losses caused to either party through the other calling off the engagement may well become the subject of a legal wrangle. This usually takes the form of a claim for any debts incurred towards the wedding arrangements that cannot readily be cancelled (such as the reception) and for any other expenses contracted by either party in consequence of the promise of marriage.

The man may feel justified in claiming the return of the engagement ring he has bought his fiancée, and for the return of any other valuable pieces of jewellery that he may have presented to her on the understanding that she was to become his wife, especially if they are family heirlooms.

The claims of either party would only have substance, how-ever, if it could be proved that they were incurred solely because of the wedding and represented nothing more than a financial loss because of the declared intention of one or other of them not to proceed with the marriage.

Damages for breach of promise are unlikely to succeed today and, consequently, the prospect of being able to heal a broken heart with a nice fat cheque is too remote to be worth even thinking about – and surely, to suffer a broken engagement is far, far better than to become the unwanted partner in an unhappy marriage?

3

PRELIMINARY REQUIREMENTS

Provided that the couple fulfil the legal qualifications set out in Chapter 1, they then decide on the form their marriage is to take.

Basically, they have the choice of being married:

1. In accordance with the rites of the Church of England;
2. In accordance with the rites of any other religious denomination;
3. Before a superintendent registrar in accordance with the Civil Law and without any religious service.

Church of England

Those who wish to be married according to the rites of this church will find that the venue of the marriage must be in the parish where the couple reside, or if they belong to different parishes, in the parish church of either one of them. Baptism is not a requirement for either partner unless the marriage is to take place by common or by special licence (where it is actually a requirement for the licence rather than for the marriage itself). The Church of England recognises all baptism by the pouring (not sprinkling) of, or immersion in, water, provided it is in the name of the Holy Trinity. Baptism for the sole purpose of matrimony is not encouraged, and it is recommended that adult baptism should not take place without the expectation of confirmation.

Custom decrees that weddings are solemnised in the parish church of the bride, though this is a matter of tradition and not of law. It is a convenient custom too, as apart from the symbolism of the man coming to collect his bride, it gives her a chance to say farewell to her friends if she is going elsewhere to live, and it makes the question of arrangements for the reception afterwards a simpler matter for the bride's parents.

It might happen, however, that one or other of the couple have been in the habit of worshipping in a church outside the parish in which he or she lives. In such a case the wedding may be conducted in that church so long as the party concerned has worshipped there regularly for not less than six months. This entitles the party concerned to sign the electoral roll of the parish (provided he/she is baptised), giving them the right of membership – including the right to be married there. If there are other reasons for wishing to marry in another church, a Special Licence is needed.

There are four ways in which marriage can be authorised to take place in a church of the Church of England:

(a) **by Banns;**
(b) **by Common Licence;**
(c) **by Special Licence;**
(d) **by a Certificate issued by a superintendent registrar.**

(a) The most usual procedure is by the reading of the banns on three Sundays in the parish church of each of the engaged couple, and in the parish where one of them is on the electoral roll, if this is the situation.

Naturally, an application must be made to the incumbent of the church in which the couple desire to be married. Only one of them need make the application. If the clergyman is satisfied that the couple are legally qualified to marry, he will arrange to give notice of their intention to the members of his congregation at one of the services on each of the Sundays concerned, permitting anyone who may have reason to doubt their qualifications to make an objection.

The banns must, of course, be read in the parish church of both the man and the woman, if they reside in different parishes – and they must continue to reside in their particular parishes for the whole of the three weeks during which the banns are read. They must *in addition* be read in the parish church where one or other of them is on the electoral roll if the marriage is to take place there.

The clergyman due to perform the ceremony will require a certificate from the clergyman of the parish church or churches of each of the couple if they are to marry elsewhere, certifying that the banns have in fact been published there too and that no valid objection has been received.

After the banns have been read for the three specified Sundays without any substantial objection being voiced, the marriage can be solemnised at any time between 8am and 6pm on any day thereafter, though the Church discourages weddings during Lent. However, there is a time limit of three calendar months to the effectiveness of this authority – and the banns must again be called if the wedding is still intended to take place after this time.

(b) Marriage by Common Licence is usually where the three weeks' delay taken up in the reading of the banns is, for some reason or another, not tolerable or where one or other party is not a British subject, or not an English or Welsh resident. The reasons for haste may be legion: a hurried move abroad by the groom or bride to take up a post overseas perhaps, or maybe because of family illness, or even perhaps because a birth is imminent.

Nor are residential qualifications so strict. Only one of the couple need live in the parish where the marriage is to be conducted, and he or she need only have resided in the parish for fifteen days immediately prior to the application. The other party to the marriage is not called upon to produce any residential qualification.

Alternatively, if one of the parties is entered on the church electoral roll that is sufficient qualification in itself. This is useful, for example, where one (or both) of the couple is temporarily working abroad and therefore cannot fulfil the residential qualifications but wishes to return home to get married.

The application for such a licence may be made to the incumbent of the church where it is desired to hold the wedding. If he is not able to grant the licence himself, he will be able to advise the couple of the address of the nearest Surrogate or the Diocesan Registrar for granting Marriage Licences in the Diocese.

The application must be made in person though only one of the parties to the wedding need do so; there is no need for both to go. To be married by Common or Special Licence (see below) at least one of the couple must be baptised and neither should be divorced with a former spouse still living. Once the licence is granted the marriage must take place within three calendar months; thereafter a new application would have to be made.

(c) Marriage by Special Licence is unusual and such a licence is only issued on the authority of the Archbishop of Canterbury through the Faculty Office (see Appendix for address).

Such a licence would only be granted when a normal legal preliminary is not possible. It is required when neither of the couple has residential qualifications, or, less often, when the ceremony is to be held in a church not licensed for marriages; perhaps by a bedside in a hospital or a home where there is a serious illness – to the point of death.

(d) It is possible to obtain a certificate of authorisation for a marriage to be conducted in a church of the Church of England from a superintendent registrar but this would not be binding on the incumbent who might well insist on a Common Licence being procured or banns called.

In any event, it would seem wise to consult the clergyman of the church first – since he may find it difficult because of prior commitments to find a suitable time for the ceremony. However, if the clergyman is willing to accept such a certificate, no further legal authorisation would be needed.

Such an application needs to be made to the superintendent registrar not less than twenty-one clear days before the wedding is expected to take place and each of the parties to it must have been resident for not less than seven days in their own district immediately before the notice is entered by the registrar. At least one party should be resident in the parish where the marriage is to take place or be on the relevant church electoral roll. (If each of the couple live in different registration districts each one must give notice in their own area.)

Once the certificate has been issued it is valid for twelve calendar months; if the wedding is to take place after that time, a new application must be made to the registrar.

The cost of a superintendent registrar's certificate is dependent on whether the couple reside in the same district or in different ones. Full details of all the various fees that relate to the different ways of being married can be obtained from the local register office.

A clergyman is under a duty to ensure that a couple is prepared for marriage, and may insist that some time be spent with him discussing the Church's teaching on how people are to 'discharge aright their obligations as married persons' (in the words of canon law). Indeed, it is also becoming more and more common to find short preparation courses for those about to marry run by non-clerical bodies (see page 30).

Other Denominations

The Roman Catholic Church

A Roman Catholic may marry another Roman Catholic, a member of another Christian church, a member of another faith, or someone with no faith affiliation at all, provided that both are free to marry. 'Free to marry' means that neither partner to the proposed marriage has been married before; or that any previous marriage of one or both has been declared invalid according to the appropriate procedures of the Roman Catholic Church.

All couples marrying in a Catholic church must obtain certificates from the superintendent registrar of marriages of the district in which they will marry – the same district in which they will have fulfilled the registrar's qualification of residency. It is presumed that at least one of the partners is resident in the district where the marriage will take place. A partner who lives in another district must obtain a certificate from the registrar of the district in which he or she lives and present that to the priest. Provided that both partners live in the same registration district, only one of the parties need attend personally on the registrar.

The Roman Catholic Church does not recognise that civil divorce brings the union of marriage to an end, but acknowledges that divorce only as a legal instrument on which decisions relating to responsibilities can be made. A second marriage while a former spouse is still living is possible only if the first marriage has been judged to have been invalid according to criteria of validity established by the Roman Catholic Church. Such cases would exist when a declaration of nullity of the previous marriage had been granted to one of the persons by a Roman Catholic Marriage Tribunal, or if a previous marriage had not complied with Church Law for its validity. In these circumstances, the couple should consult their parish priest at the earliest opportunity.

If the engaged couple live in different districts, notice must be given to the superintendent registrar in both, and to establish their residential qualifications, they must each have resided in the district where his or her application is to be made for at least seven days prior to the notice being entered by the registrar. Twenty-one days thereafter the superintendent registrar will issue the required Certificates – provided that neither notice has resulted in valid objections being raised.

Where it is desired to hold the wedding ceremony within the prescribed twenty-one days after the entry of the notice, the superintendent registrar may issue a superintendent registrar's Licence together with his Certificate. This entitles the couple to marry at any time after the elapse of one clear working day after the notice has been given.

Where a superintendent registrar's Licence is sought, only one of the engaged couple need have residential qualifications, but that person must have lived for not less than fifteen days continuously in the district where the application is made, immediately prior to the notice being given to the registrar.

It is well to consult the parish priest concerning the detailed arrangements for the wedding since, although the registrar's Certificate authorises the marriage under the civil law, it does not insist that the church shall carry out the ceremony. The Roman Catholic Church still requires that banns be read in the parish church of each of the betrothed – except in the event of one of them not being a Catholic. In such a case, no banns are read. There are differing types of service to solemnise matrimony too, dependent upon whether one or other of the parties is a non-Catholic.

Generally speaking, a Catholic priest will require up to six

months' notice of a projected wedding, and longer if possible.
This will enable him to provide for adequate preparation of the
couple. Nowadays in most Catholic churches this is regarded as
essential, and not only where one of the parties is a non-Catholic.

Marriage Care (formerly the Catholic Marriage Advisory
Council) help to provide 'Preparation for Marriage' courses
throughout the country. These courses are arranged locally either
by the parish churches or by the Marriage Care centre and
information about them can be obtained either from the local
church itself or the local centre. Telephone numbers of centres in
England and Wales and in Scotland are held by Marriage Care
(see Appendix for address and telephone number).

A couple planning a wedding in a Catholic church should
check with the priest that the building is registered for marriages
and whether or not an 'authorised person' will be in attendance
(see under Free Churches, below). Many Roman Catholic priests
are registered or authorised persons.

Free Churches
Adequate notice is also required by the ministers of the various
Free Churches such as the Methodists, Baptists and the United
Reformed Church (which includes most Presbyterian and Con-
gregationalist churches) of marriages intended to be celebrated in
their churches.

To comply with the civil law all marriages must take place
within a church or a building registered by the Registrar General
for the purpose of conducting marriage services. Such marriages
must be witnessed by at least two people who have reached the
age of 18 and by an 'authorised person', i.e. the registrar, his
deputy or, more usually, a minister (or member) of the church
who has been authorised by the Registrar General.

Many of the Free and Roman Catholic churches are registered
under the Marriage Acts but some are not; most of the clergymen
of these churches are 'authorised', but by no means all of them. It
is obviously important to check on these points because the
couple may need to arrange for a civil ceremony to take place in
a register office when applying to the superintendent registrar for
a certificate.

Where the building is registered but the minister performing the ceremony is not an 'authorised person', or cannot arrange for such a person to be present, the couple should inform the superintendent registrar of the need for a registrar's presence at the church. The fact that a minister is not an authorised person does not preclude him from conducting the marriage service, but it does require the attendance of some other person authorised for the area or the registrar or his deputy to oversee the legal side of the proceedings. The minister will usually be able to arrange for an authorised person to attend where he is not himself authorised or will advise when a registrar will be needed. If there is any doubt, these details should be checked with the minister of the church where the wedding is to take place.

The conditions attached to the issue of a Superintendent Registrar's Certificate or Licence are described elsewhere in this chapter and need not be repeated.

The Jewish religion
The civil law is varied in the case of a Jewish wedding to permit the ceremony to take place anywhere: in a synagogue, a private house, a hired hall, or any chosen place, whether registered for the purpose or not. There are no times specified during which the service must be held – though it is usual for the ceremony to be performed in a synagogue at any convenient time, excluding the hours between sunset on Friday and sunset the following day (Saturday), the Jewish Sabbath. Marriages do not take place, though, on any festival or intermediate days of any festival; on any Fast day; in the three weeks from the Fast of Tammuz to the Fast of Av; and certain weeks during the counting of the Omer. It is unusual for marriages to take place on the eves of Sabbaths or Festivals. For full details, consult your Rabbi or Secretary of the Synagogue.

A Quaker wedding (Religious Society of Friends)
A Quaker wedding requires, of course, the same recourse to a superintendent registrar for a Certificate or Licence, as in all cases save those of the Church of England. It requires, too, the completion of the Society's own marriage forms.

Marriage according to Quaker usage is subject to approval by their Registering Officers acting for the meeting concerned. The Registering Officer will give advice and information, and is responsible for issuing the forms and registering the marriage.

Quaker marriage is not an alternative form of marriage available to the general public but is restricted to members and those associated with them. Therefore at least one of the parties must be known to a local Quaker meeting and be in unity with the Quaker religious nature and witness.

A non-member of the Society will need to have the written support of two adult members who are satisfied that he/she is in agreement with the Quaker view of marriage.

Notice of the intended marriage is given at the close of the Sunday morning meetings where the parties are members or where they usually worship, or in the district where they live.

If no written notice of objection is received, the Registering Officer completes a form to this effect and arrangements for the wedding can then proceed.

Civil ceremony
There is no need for a marriage to be solemnised by a minister of religion. Only the civil law need be heeded and such a marriage in a register office or other approved premises, conducted by a superintendent registrar, is as completely binding in law as any conducted under the auspices of a religious body.

There are many reasons why a couple may elect to be married with a civil ceremony: they may subscribe to no religious beliefs; they may be of different denominational persuasions and prefer to marry under a neutral, secular authority; they may be debarred by the church because one or both have been divorced; the church or chapel in which they wish to hold the religious service may not be registered for marriages.

Absolute secrecy is not, of course, possible, as the intention to marry is published by an entry in the superintendent registrar's 'notice book' which is available for all to inspect. Also, all notices are exhibited on the superintendent registrar's notice board.

For such a marriage, notice must be given to the superintendent registrar in the district(s) where the couple live. Notice must be given in person and a detailed application form must be completed. The couple can be married in any register office or approved premises in England and Wales.

The person giving notice must state the names, ages and addresses of each party (with the period each has resided there), along with details of their marital status, occupation, and where the marriage is to take place. A declaration must also be made stating that there is no lawful impediment to the marriage.

If either of the parties is under 18 years of age, and marrying for the first time, the written consent of both parents or other legal guardians is required.

For marriage by Superintendent Registrar's Certificate both parties to the marriage must have lived in a registration district in England or Wales for at least seven days immediately preceding the giving of notice at the register office. If the couple live in the same registration district, only one party need give notice; if the couple live in different districts, separate notice must be made in each district. If either of the parties has been married previously, he or she will have to produce proof to the superintendent registrar, either in the form of a death certificate or a decree absolute, that there is no legal barrier to a second marriage.

If no objection is received and verified within twenty-one clear days of the entry of notice, the superintendent registrar will issue his Certificate and the marriage can be conducted as soon thereafter as is convenient.

If, for some reason or other, the couple wish to be married within the prescribed twenty-one days, they may apply to the superintendent registrar for marriage by Licence (sometimes known as 'special licence'). The conditions for its issue are similar to those required for the Certificate, except that only one of the parties must meet a residential qualification and must have lived in a registration district in England or Wales for at least fifteen days before giving notice at the register office. The second party to the marriage only needs to be a resident of, or be physically in, England or Wales on the day notice is given.

If there is no objection, the Licence for marriage will be issued after the expiry of one clear working day (excluding a Sunday,

Christmas Day or Good Friday) from the entry of the notice, and the marriage can take place any time thereafter.

Once issued, a notice for marriage – by Certificate or Licence – is valid for one year. (Before 1 October 1997 it was only valid for three months.) However, if any unforeseen delays prevent the ceremony taking place as planned, the couple should check their position with the local register office for clarification.

In order for the couple to secure their choice of venue, date and time for their marriage ceremony it is usually possible for an advance (provisional) booking to be made with the superintendent registrar of the district in which they wish the ceremony to take place. Again, the register office in the district in question would be able to give more precise information in this respect. If such an advance booking is made, the couple must still remember to give formal notice to their own superintendent registrar(s) in due course in order to complete the legal formalities without which a marriage cannot take place.

Since 1995, when the 1994 Marriage Act (England and Wales) became law, civil marriage ceremonies have not been restricted to register offices. Any building approved for civil marriage can be used, and a complete list of such premises is available from the office of the Registrar General in Southport, for a fee (see Appendix for address). Any register office would be able to supply a list of local approved premises but the full list, covering the whole of England and Wales, is only available from the office of the Registrar General.

Perhaps the biggest advantage with using an approved premises other than a register office is that usually there will be more time available for the ceremony and therefore the couple will have greater freedom to personalise it. Couples can discuss the ceremony with the superintendent registrar. The legal element is the same as the register office but readings, music, etc. can be added. The only restriction is that there must be no religious element to the proceedings.

Once the venue has been chosen an appointment should be made with the register office of that district to discuss the necessary arrangements. Two registrars will need to attend the ceremony (one to conduct the ceremony and one to register the marriage), so a date should not be confirmed with the chosen venue until double checked with the relevant register office. The couple will have to apply for a Superintendent Registrar's Certificate from the district(s) where they each live and present it to the superintendent registrar in the district where the marriage is to take place, if different. (The above does not apply in Scotland, where the civil ceremony must still take place within a register office.)

While the fees for giving notice to the superintendent registrar and for the registrar's attendance at a marriage at a register office are set nationally, the fee for attendance of the superintendent registrar and registrar at a marriage in approved premises is set by the local authority. The local register office should therefore be consulted with regard to the fees for a civil wedding.

Serving members of the Royal Navy
Serving members of the Royal Navy who are sea-going are not penalised by their inability to establish residential qualifications ashore. In any such case the sailor may make application to his Captain to have the banns read aboard his ship during morning service on three successive Sundays; the banns also being read in the bride's church, where the ceremony will eventually take place, at the same time.

At the end of the qualifying period of twenty-one days, the Captain will make an entry in his Banns of Marriage Register and issue a certificate stating that the banns have been called and that no valid objections to the marriage have been brought to his attention. This certificate must then be passed to the clergyman ashore who is to perform the wedding ceremony.

When it is intended that the marriage should take place before a superintendent registrar, or before a clergyman of a church other than one of the Church of England, the seaman should complete a form of notice in the presence of his Captain and that officer should countersign it as a witness. After twenty-one days, the Captain will issue a certificate informing the superintendent registrar that due notice was given to him by the seaman, and that no valid objection had been brought to his notice.

As soon as the bridegroom's certificate has been issued, the bride must give similar notice to the superintendent registrar in the district where she lives and where the marriage is to be conducted, and to the officiating clergyman if a church service is intended.

Marriage preparation courses

The aim of any marriage preparation course is for the engaged couple to learn more about themselves and each other. In this way they will be better prepared for marriage and for working together through the ups and downs of married life.

The content of such courses may vary according to who is running them. Clergyman will want to be sure that details of the service are clear, and that the church's teaching on marriage is understood by each of the engaged couple so that they may make their vows with conviction. However, like many of the lay courses on offer, they will probably also want to look beyond the marriage service itself to the relationship of each individual couple.

By exploring attitudes to love and sex, family, finances, work, religion, personality, communication and many other topics, a couple can discuss with an objective third party the strengths and areas for growth in their relationship. Very often these courses prompt discussion of issues that may never otherwise have been discussed. Being aware of how to discuss difficult subjects and potential problems before they arise can give a couple the means to meet and overcome troubles that occur along life's path.

It would be well worthwhile for any couple contemplating marriage to attend a preparation course and details about courses should be available from most clergymen, or most libraries should stock the Directory of Marriage Support Services providers (which will include practitioners of the Prepare/Enrich Network UK). Alternatively the Lord Chancellor's Department at Selbourne House, London, will be able to advise where this Directory may be consulted (see Appendix for address).

4

NORTHERN IRELAND AND SCOTLAND

Marriage regulations and laws are different in Northern Ireland and Scotland.

NORTHERN IRELAND

Requirement to Give Notification of Intention to Marry

Any person marrying in Ireland, either by a religious or a civil ceremony, must give three months' notice of intention to marry to the registrar for the district in which the marriage is to take place. This is in addition to any other preliminaries which are legally required according to the particular form the marriage service is to take.

Notification of a marriage may be given in one of two ways:

(a) The couple may write jointly (or separately) to the registrar for the district in which the marriage is to be solemnised, giving the name and address of the parties to the marriage, the name of the church or place where the marriage is to take place, the date on which the marriage is to take place and the age of the parties or confirmation that the parties are over eighteen.

(b) The couple may complete and return to the registrar a pre-printed form, available from the registrar.

(If only one letter or form is sent to the registrar it must be signed by each of the couple.)

The registrar will issue each of the couple with an acknow-ledgement confirming the date of receipt of the notification which should be kept safely and given to the person solemnising the marriage on request.

If for some reason the provision of three months' notification of intention to marry causes difficulties, application could be made to Court for an exemption and the Court will decide whether or not the marriage should proceed. Such applications should be made through the Circuit Family Court Office or the High Court Office in the area where the marriage is to take place. One of these offices should be contacted for exact details of how to go about such an application but the procedure is an informal one. Each of the couple must make the application and may apply in person without employing the services of a solicitor. There is no charge for such an application.

The Court will expect each applicant to show that the application is justified on valid and substantive grounds and also that the granting of such an application is in the interest of the parties to the intended marriage. If the Court does not give permission the marriage cannot take place.

The minimum age for marriage in Ireland is 16 although anyone under 18 must have the written consent on a prescribed form (normally completed by both parents) or, if appropriate, an order of a court dispensing with consent. Evidence of age must be given if requested by a registrar or any person to whom an application is made for a Licence, Certificate or the publication of banns, or by the person who is to solemnise the marriage. A marriage will not be recognised as valid in Irish law if one of the parties is under 18 years of age, wherever the marriage has taken place, unless parental consent or court exemption has been granted to allow the marriage to proceed. (Applications for exemptions should be made in the same way as described above for those seeking permission to marry without giving three months' notification.)

For civil marriages and marriages according to the rites and ceremonies of any denomination other than the Roman Catholic Church, the registrar to whom notification should be given is the Registrar of Civil Marriages for the district in which the marriage is to be solemnised. For marriages according to the rites and ceremonies of the Roman Catholic Church, the registrar to whom notification should be given is the Registrar of Births, Deaths and (Roman Catholic) Marriages for the district in which the marriage is to be solemnised.

Documents and witnesses
If the couple can produce their birth certificates at the time when notice of marriage is given this is helpful to the registrar. Also, anyone who has been married previously should produce documentation or evidence of the death of the former spouse or the dissolution or annulment of the previous marriage. For marriages where one of the parties is from abroad, an official travel or identity document for that person should be produced. Photocopies of documents are not acceptable unless certified to be a true copy by the issuing authority.

At all marriages there must be present two witnesses to the marriage who must sign the marriage register. It is for the engaged couple to arrange the presence of these witnesses.

Church of Ireland
A marriage may be authorised to take place in a church of the Church of Ireland in four different ways:

(a) by Banns;
(b) by Licence;
(c) by Special Licence;
(d) by a Certificate issued by a registrar.

(a) Where both parties to the marriage are members of the Church of Ireland or other Protestant Episcopal Church, banns may be published in the church of the parish in which the parties live. (If they live in different parishes, banns must be published in both.) Seven days' notice to the minister(s) may be required and publication must be made on three Sundays or Feast days before the date of the marriage. The marriage ceremony must then take place in the church (or one of the churches) in which the banns have been published. The clergyman who is to conduct the service must be consulted about the arrangements.

(b) To obtain a Licence, one or both of the parties to the

marriage must be members of the Church of Ireland or other Protestant Episcopal Church. The Licence is obtainable from a Church of Ireland licensing minister for a marriage in a church within their district. One of the parties must have resided for at least seven days in the licensing minister's district immediately before giving notice of the intended marriage. If a Licence can be granted it will be granted seven days after notice is received and the licensing minister will send copies of the notice to the clergymen of the places of worship which the parties normally attend.

Immediately before the grant of the Licence, one of the parties must make an oath or declaration which includes a clause to the effect that one of them has lived for the past fourteen days within the district attached to the church in which they intend to marry.

The name and address of a District Church of Ireland Licenser can be obtained from any Church of Ireland clergyman.

(c) A Special Licence may be granted by a Bishop of the Church of Ireland, provided one or both of the parties to the marriage are members of that church or other Protestant Episcopal Church. This authorises the marriage to take place at any time and in any place within the Bishop's diocese.

(d) A registrar's Certificate may be obtained, where one or both of the parties are members of the Church of Ireland or other Protestant Episcopal Church, authorising the marriage to take place in a church. The application for the Certificate must be made to the registrar in the district where the couple live. If they live in different registration districts a Certificate must be obtained from the registrar in each district. Whether or not they live in different districts each of the couple must have lived in their district(s) for at least seven days immediately before giving notice to the registrar. (If they live in the same district it does not matter which of the couple gives notice.) After twenty-one clear days from the date that the notice was given, the registrar may issue his Certificate. The registrar(s) must send copies of the notice of marriage to the ministers of the places of worship usually attended by the couple, and, if different from either of these, to the minister of the church where the marriage is to be held.

At least one of the parties must have resided in the district attached to the church where the marriage is to be celebrated for fourteen days immediately before the marriage.

Presbyterian Churches
Marriages according to the form and discipline of various Presbyterian bodies may take place by:

(a) **Licence;**
(b) **Special Licence;**
(c) **Banns.**

The governing bodies concerned are:

(a) The General Assembly of the Presbyterian Church in Ireland.
(b) The Remonstrant Synod of Ulster (*non-subscribing*).
(c) The Presbytery of Antrim.
(d) The Reformed Presbyterian Synod of Ireland.

Though the form and discipline may differ somewhat, the authorisation for the celebration of marriage is similar. (In the case of the Evangelical Presbyterian Church and the Free Presbyterian Church the procedure is as with *Other Denominations* set out later.)

(a) To obtain a Licence, which is the normal procedure, one or both of the parties must be of the particular Presbyterian Church involved. Application must first be made to the minister of the congregation of which one of them has been a member for at least the past month. He will then issue a certificate confirming that notice has been given which must be produced by (one of) the couple to the licensing minister. Seven days after the receipt of the certificate, the licensing minister may issue the Licence authorising the marriage. The Licence must be produced to the officiating minister before the marriage service takes place.

Immediately before the grant of the Licence, whichever of the couple gave notice to the licensing minister must make a declaration (or oath) which includes a statement to the effect that one of the parties has resided for the past fifteen days within the presbytery. (Regular connection with a congregation of the presbytery may sometimes be taken as a 'residential' qualification.)

(b) A Special Licence authorising marriage at any time or place in Ireland may be granted by the Moderator of one of the governing bodies mentioned above. One or both of the engaged couple must be a member of a congregation of the church body presided over by the Moderator granting the Special Licence.

(c) Where both parties to the marriage are members of the same Presbyterian body, banns may be published in the church or churches of which they are members. The minister(s) concerned will (each) require six days' notice and publication must be made on three Sundays before the marriage. The ceremony must take place in the church (or one of the churches) in which the banns have been published.

It is not legal to publish banns where one of the parties is a member of another church body or the wedding is to take place in the church of another body.

It must be emphasised, as indicated above, that for banns both parties must be members of the same Presbyterian denomination (not just both Presbyterians but of different church bodies) even when these are in full mutual relationship. This must be emphasised because almost all the requests that come to the ministers for the calling of banns come from other denominations, in Ireland or Britain, where this is the normal procedure.

The Roman Catholic Church
Marriages according to the rites and ceremonies of the Roman Catholic Church may be solemnised:

(a) by Episcopal Licence;
(b) after publication of banns;
(c) by Licence;
(d) by a Certificate issued by a Registrar of Marriages.

(a) and **(b)**: Both parties must be Roman Catholic. The proceedings are regulated by the law of the Roman Catholic Church and the parties should apply to their parish priest or priests for information about the steps to be taken.

(c) For marriage by Licence, one or both of the parties must be Roman Catholic. A Licence may be obtained from a licenser appointed by a Bishop of the Roman Catholic Church. Where only one party is Roman Catholic notice must be given to the licenser seven days before the issue of the Licence and the licenser must send copies of the notice to the clergymen of the place of worship which each party regularly attends.

(d) A registrar's Certificate may authorise a marriage in a Roman Catholic church within the registration district between a Roman Catholic and a person who is not a Roman Catholic. This method is not available if both parties are Roman Catholic. Both parties must have lived in their own registration district for at least seven days immediately before giving notice to the registrar of that district. If they live in the same district, notice may be given by either party; if they live in different districts each must give notice to the registrar of their own district. The registrar(s) must send copies of the notice to the ministers of the places of worship usually attended by the couple, and to the minister of the church where the marriage is to be held (if different). After twenty-one clear days from the date that notice was given the registrar may issue his Certificate. Where notice was given in different districts a Certificate must be issued by each registrar.

Other Denominations
(including Baptists, Brethren, Congregationalists, Free Presbyterians, Methodists, Salvation Army, Jews and the Society of Friends, etc.)

Three forms of authorisation for a marriage are available to the members of other religious bodies:

(a) **by Registrar's Certificate;**
(b) **by Registrar's Licence (except for Jews and members of the Society of Friends);**
(c) **by Special Licence (in certain cases).**

(For some denominations the registrar must be present at the marriage ceremony. In such circumstances the parties are advised to agree the proposed time and date of the ceremony with the registrar well in advance before finalising their arrangements. Further information about this may be obtained from the registrar.)

(a) A registrar's Certificate may authorise a marriage in a register office, a church or other registered building in his district provided that at least one of the engaged couple lives in that district. Both parties must have lived in their own registration district(s) for at least seven days immediately before giving notice to the registrar of that district. If they live in the same district, notice may be given by either party; if they live in different districts each must give notice to the registrar of their own district. The registrar(s) must send copies of the notice to the ministers of the place of worship usually attended by each of the couple, and to the minister of the church where the marriage is to be held (if different). After twenty-one clear days from the date that notice was given the registrar may issue his Certificate. Where notice was given in different districts a Certificate must be issued by each registrar.

(b) A registrar's Licence may authorise a marriage in a register office, church or other building registered for marriages in the registration district, provided that at least one of the parties lives in that district. Under the Licence a marriage can be solemnised seven clear days after the date of notice, instead of the twenty-one clear days required under a registrar's Certificate.

If both parties reside in the same registrar's district, one must have resided there for not less than fifteen days and the other for not less than seven days immediately before notice is given to the registrar in that district. If one of the parties resides in another district, notice must be given to the registrar of each district and both parties must have lived in their respective districts for fifteen days immediately before giving notice.

The registrar(s) must send copies of the notice to the ministers of the place or worship usually attended by each of the couple, and to the minister of the church where the marriage is to be held (if different). The registrar of the district in which the marriage is to take place will require the certificate from the registrar of the other district before he will issue his Licence. Seven clear days after the giving of notice, and after administering an oath or declaration to one of the parties including a clause to the effect that one of the couple has lived within the district in which they intend to marry for fifteen days immediately prior to the grant of the Licence, the registrar may issue the Licence.

(c) Marriage by Special Licence, which may be celebrated at any time and at any place in Ireland, is an option available to Baptists, Congregationalists, Methodists and members of the Society of Friends. One or both of the engaged couple must be members of the same church as the person who grants the Special Licence. Such a Licence may be granted by the President of the Association of Baptist Churches in Ireland, the Secretary of the Conference of the Methodist Church in Ireland or the Clerk of the Yearly Meeting of the Society of Friends in Ireland.

Jews

Marriages according to the customs of Jews may take place only by registrar's certificate but need not be celebrated within the district of residence of either party.

Civil Marriages

Where a couple desire to be married without any religious ceremony, they may apply to a registrar to be married in his office. There are twenty-six District Councils in Northern Ireland, each with its own registration office. The address of the local registrar can be found in the telephone directory under 'Registration'. The marriages must take place by the registrar's Licence or registrar's Certificate as described above under *Other Denominations*.

Registrar General's Licence

The Registrar General may issue a Licence allowing a marriage between a couple, one of whom is either house-bound or detained as a prisoner or as a patient under the Mental Health (Northern Ireland) Order 1986, to be solemnised at the residence of the person who is house-bound or detained. Notice of marriage must be given by one of the parties to the registrar of the district in which the marriage is to be solemnised. If the parties live in different districts, notice must be given to the registrar of each district. Further information about the requirements can be obtained from the registrar.

The Registrar General's Licence cannot be issued for a marriage according to the rites of the Roman Catholic Church between two persons professing the Roman Catholic religion, according to the customs of the Jews between two people professing the Jewish religion or according to the customs of the Society of Friends.

Where One of the Parties is Resident Outside Northern Ireland

In the case of a marriage pursuant to the Licence of a Church of Ireland or Presbyterian Licenser, if one party resides in Northern Ireland and fulfils the statutory conditions, that party can take all the steps necessary to obtain the Licence, and the residence of the other party is immaterial.

For a marriage in a church of the Church of Ireland in Northern Ireland, when both parties are Protestant Episcopalians and one of them resides in England or Wales, it is lawful for banns to be published in respect of the latter party in the parish or place of residence in England and Wales, banns being also duly published in the parish or district of residence of the party living in Northern Ireland.

In the case of an intended marriage in Northern Ireland for which authority from a registrar is required, and where one of the parties resides in England or Wales, the party so resident should serve notice to, and (seven days afterwards) obtain a Certificate from the superintendent registrar of the district of residence. Seven days after the issue of such a Certificate it becomes valid for the purpose of marriage in Northern Ireland. It should be given to the registrar in Northern Ireland who may issue his authority for the marriage provided that the party living in his district has also taken the necessary steps there.

If notice is given for marriage by registrar's Certificate the authority cannot be issued until twenty-one days from the date that notice was given.

Where one of the engaged couple lives in Scotland and is a

member of the Church of Scotland that party may get banns read on three successive Sundays in his or her own church and receive a certificate from the minister stating that this has occurred. After seven days that certificate becomes valid for the purpose of marriage in Northern Ireland. It should be given to the registrar there who may issue his authority for the marriage provided that the party living in his district has taken the required steps there. The certificate regarding banns is not required if the marriage is to take place by Licence issued by a licensing minister or by Special Licence.

If the party living in Scotland is not a member of the Church of Scotland they would have to establish appropriate residence in Northern Ireland before notice of marriage may be given (see registrar's Certificate and registrar's Licence, above).

Where the Marriage is to Take Place in Great Britain (not Northern Ireland)

Where a marriage is to be solemnised in England or Wales by the 'certificate' procedure and one of the parties resides in Northern Ireland, the party resident in Northern Ireland should serve notice on the registrar of the district where he or she resides and obtain the registrar's Certificate for production to the superintendent registrar of the district in England or Wales where the marriage is to take place. (A registrar's Licence cannot be granted where the marriage is to take place outside Northern Ireland.) Where the marriage is intended to take place in a church of the Church of England, it is within the power of the incumbent to refuse to act upon such a Certificate, and his prior consent should accordingly be obtained. The party resident in England or Wales must also take the requisite steps there. For further information contact the General Register Office in Southport (see Appendix for address).

If the marriage is to take place in Scotland, the party resident in Northern Ireland is not required to give notice to the registrar in Northern Ireland. Neither of the parties need to have resided in Scotland before notice is given to the registrar there and notice may be given either in person or by post. It is recommended that at least six weeks before the date of the marriage enquiries should be made with the Scottish registrar in whose district the marriage is to take place. Further information about marriage in Scotland may be obtained from the General Register Office for Scotland (see Appendix for address).

SCOTLAND

There are several differences between the marriage laws of England and Wales, and Scotland:

(a) Where the banns must be read in a church of the Church of England on three successive Sundays, banns are no longer required for a religious marriage in Scotland.

(b) Residence is not a requirement but both parties to a marriage, whether religious or civil, must give at the very least fifteen days' notice before the date of the proposed marriage.

(c) In Scotland, as in the rest of the United Kingdom, the legal minimum age for marriage is 16, but parental consent is not required by law in Scotland for those under 18 years of age.

Each of the parties must complete and submit a marriage notice, which can be obtained from any registrar of births, deaths and marriages in Scotland. (The local address will be found in the telephone book.) The following documents will need to be taken or sent with the appropriate fee to the registrar for the district in which the marriage is to take place: birth certificate; copy of the decree of divorce or annulment if there has been a previous marriage (a decree nisi is not acceptable); and, for widows or widowers, the death certificate of the former spouse.

Timing is most important. The marriage notices must be submitted early enough to enable the registrar to satisfy himself that the couple are free to marry one another. He should have the notices four weeks before the marriage, but if either party has been married before, the registrar should receive the notices six weeks beforehand.

Every person giving notice has to sign a declaration that the particulars and information they have given on the marriage notice are correct. As a safeguard against bigamous marriages a subsequent check of the information is made centrally.

When he is satisfied there is no legal impediment to the marriage, the registrar will prepare a Marriage Schedule from the information given to him. This Schedule is most important – no marriage can proceed without it.

If it is to be a religious wedding the Marriage Schedule will be issued to the couple by the registrar. It cannot be issued more than seven days before the marriage and the couple will be told when to call for it. The Schedule cannot be collected by a relative or friend, it will only be issued to the prospective bride or bridegroom. The Marriage Schedule *must* be produced before the marriage ceremony to the person performing the marriage.

Immediately after the religious ceremony the Marriage Schedule must be signed by the bride and bridegroom, by the person performing the marriage and by two witnesses who are aged 16 or over. It must then be returned to the registrar within three days so that he can register the marriage.

If it is to be a civil marriage, the Marriage Schedule will not be issued to the couple but the registrar will have it at the marriage ceremony for signature. Subsequently he can register the marriage. A fee for the civil marriage is payable to the registrar in advance. After the marriage has been registered, copies of the marriage certificate can be obtained from the registrar on payment of the appropriate fee. (For advice on all fees, contact the local register office.)

Marriage via a Religious Service
A religious marriage, whether Christian or non-Christian (Jewish, Moslem, Hindu, etc.) may be solemnised only by a minister, clergyman, pastor, priest or other person entitled to do so under the Marriage (Scotland) Act 1977. Couples wishing to be married during a religious service should go and see the person who is to conduct the ceremony before completing the notice of marriage.

Civil Marriages
The procedures have been detailed in the preceding paragraphs.

One or Both Parties Live in England or Wales
If one of the parties to the marriage lives in Scotland, or both live in England or Wales but one has a parent living in Scotland, notice of the wedding should be given to the superintendent

registrar in the district in England or Wales in which one of the parties must have lived for the preceding seven days. The other party should, however, give notice in Scotland as explained earlier. The Certificate issued by the superintendent registrar in England or Wales should be sent to the registrar in Scotland where the marriage is to be held. This Certificate will obviate the need for the partner living in England or Wales to give notice in Scotland.

One Party Lives Outside the United Kingdom

If one party lives outside the United Kingdom or has lived here for less than two years, the normal procedure of giving notice to the registrar in Scotland must be followed. In addition to the documents mentioned earlier a *certificate of no impediment* will be required, issued by the competent authority (usually the civil authority) to the effect that the party concerned is free to marry. (If any document is in a language other than English, a certified translation should also be produced.) Without this certificate it may not be possible for the marriage to go ahead.

5

MARRIAGE FOR THOSE LIVING ABROAD, FOREIGNERS, ETC.

Marriage regulations and laws are not the same for foreigners marrying in the United Kingdom, nor do they apply in quite the same way to British subjects marrying abroad. Also, where a British subject intends to marry a foreigner – abroad or at home – there is always the matter of the couple's nationality after the marriage.

The engaged couple would be well advised to consult the various authorities. In Britain an interview should be sought with a clergyman or leader of the religious denomination involved. If there is to be no religious service, advice will be available at any superintendent registrars' office, the addresses of which may be found in a local telephone directory.

If a British subject intends to marry abroad, he or she should consult a member of the British Embassy, Legation or Consulate in the country and district where the marriage is to take place, irrespective of whether both parties are British or one of them happens to be a national of the country concerned.

Similarly, a foreigner wishing to marry in the United Kingdom, whether to a British subject or to someone of their own nationality, should consult his or her resident representative in Britain to make sure that their marriage will be accepted as legally binding in their own country.

(See also page 44 regarding marriage in Scotland.)

6

THE RE-MARRIAGE OF DIVORCED PERSONS

Church of England

The Church of England expressly forbids the re-marriage of a divorced person during the lifetime of a previous partner.

A clergyman has the legal right to refuse to marry in church anyone whose previous partner is still alive, irrespective of whether the person concerned is the injured or the guilty party. Nor can he be compelled to permit such a marriage to take place in his church. Nor can he be compelled to conduct a service for anyone who has re-married under civil law. However, the clergyman also has a right under civil law to ignore Church rules and take the Marriage Service for a divorcee if he so wishes. No Common or Special Licence will be issued for such a marriage.

When the couple, one of whose marriage has previously been dissolved, is anxious to have some form of religious ceremony, most clergymen will be willing to hold a service of prayer and dedication. Although strictly speaking this service should be both quiet and private, at the discretion of the clergyman – and subject to the regulations issued by the General Synod – it can be fuller and richer although it must be made quite clear that it is *not*, in fact, a marriage service.

Roman Catholic Church

The Church of Rome does not recognise the right of the civil authorities to dissolve a marriage through divorce. In consequence, normally there can be no 're-marriage' where there is a partner surviving.

There are, however, some circumstances in which the Roman Catholic Church will not recognise the previous marriage. This will be the case when a Catholic was previously married outside the authority of the Catholic Church. It will also be verified where the Catholic authorities, in the form of the Marriage Tribunal, have declared a previous marriage to be null and void. In such cases, the Church will be prepared to marry that person – provided, of course, that he or she has the legal right in civil law by being divorced by the State from their original partner.

Free Churches
In the Free Churches the question of the re-marriage of a divorced person is very much at the discretion of each particular minister. Some of them firmly believe that the original contract is binding for life, others may accept the fact that the wronged party is being unjustly penalized and yet others will consider that everyone is entitled to another chance.

In consequence, an approach to a minister is necessary – and some couples have approached more than one minister before contacting one who is willing to marry them.

The Society of Friends
Although Quakers believe in the sanctity and life-long nature of marriage they are sympathetic to, and understanding of, those who have been divorced and wish to marry in a Friends' meeting.

Nevertheless, they are not willing to consider the question of re-marriage without all the circumstances being taken into account. The monthly meeting would need to be satisfied that the person seeking their permission was well known to them and associated with the last meeting. It is possible that the matter might be investigated by a small group of Friends so that the monthly meeting might be advised by them without the need to air all the circumstances in public.

The monthly meetings are given discretion whether or not to grant permission to those who wish to re-marry in a Friends' meeting.

Civil Re-marriages
The law of England and Wales recognises a divorced person as free to marry so long as they can produce a decree absolute.

Having produced that document, a re-marriage via a civil ceremony is conducted on exactly the same conditions as those applying to a first marriage.

Divorced Persons in Scotland

The only difference between the various regulations and conditions applying for re-marriage between England and Wales and Scotland concerns the method of divorce.

In England and Wales a decree *nisi* pronounces the divorce, but neither party is free to re-marry until a decree absolute has been obtained. This is obtainable on application by the successful petitioner, six weeks after the decree *nisi*.

In Scotland there is no such thing as a preliminary pronouncement. Once the decree of divorce is pronounced the divorced person is free to take immediate steps towards re-marriage if they should so desire.

7

OTHER ARRANGEMENTS TO BE MADE

In the previous chapters the couple will have discovered the procedures by which their marriage may be conducted – and have decided on the one most appropriate and suitable to themselves. All other arrangements must depend on the time, the date and the venue of the marriage itself.

The date
The date needs to be chosen with care. In the first place it must coincide with available dates and times at the venue where the wedding is to take place – church, register office or other approved premises – and, of course, with the agreement of the clergyman or registrar who will conduct the service.

In some areas it is difficult to book the arrangements because of the demand by other couples. Saturdays, for instance, are generally reserved for weeks (if not months) ahead as weekends are usually the most convenient times for the majority of the guests. Also, the couple's normal holidays from work usually need to coincide with the honeymoon so the summer months are a busy time for weddings. Easter and the Spring and August Bank Holidays are also popular periods and cause queues of wedding parties at churches, register offices and other approved premises up and down the land.

In any event there will generally need to be as little haste between the decision to marry and the wedding day itself as possible. Other arrangements might prove just as difficult to conclude, unless there is time in hand. But once the date and the time of the wedding have been fixed, the bride and groom – and, indeed, the bride's parents – can turn their attention to all the other arrangements that are so necessary to make a success of the occasion.

The Bridegroom

The bridegroom is traditionally least concerned in the making of the arrangements, though he can expect to be consulted by the bride on many matters, and to have to discuss with her some of his own plans.

Broadly, the bridegroom's tasks cover:

His 'stag party'.

The purchase of the wedding rings.

The planning and booking of everything in connection with the honeymoon – not forgetting passports, travellers' cheques and inoculations (if needed) and the car from the reception to the station or airport if they are to leave by train or air. Most couples choose their honeymoon destination together, but sometimes a groom likes to make all the arrangements himself and surprise his future wife!

The buying or hiring of his own wedding clothes.

The selection of his best man and ushers.

Before an offer is made, the bridegroom should consider carefully whether the proposed best man would be eager to accept the duty (you don't want someone who accepts only because he feels he has to) and whether he has the ability and enthusiasm to help carry out the detailed task of organising the event and of dealing with the practical tasks that arise.

Is he capable of making a speech without being a bore? Is he quick-witted enough to deal with an emergency – dropped wedding rings, the tension caused by a late arriving bride, getting to the church to find it locked because the clergyman has got his dates wrong? Is he responsible enough to safeguard the ring(s) and any other items under his charge (such as honeymoon tickets and passports)? Is he available to take part in the ceremony on the planned date? (Let him know as soon as it's fixed.) Is he totally reliable? You don't want someone who will let you down at the eleventh hour.

The final (and by no means small) consideration is whether he gets on with the bride well enough. Although the selection of best man is no real concern of hers, obviously the groom won't want to upset her by choosing someone whom she doesn't like.

Of course, it is possible – if highly unusual – for the 'best man' to be a woman. If the groom does choose a sister or female friend he should be sure she possesses all the characteristics listed above. Also, in these circumstances it is even more important that the bride knows about, and agrees with, his choice. It is her day, after all, and she should be free to say if she cannot cope with the idea of a female best man. Of course, some of the guests may raise an eyebrow too! The photographer, minister or registrar and all the wedding party should be informed and introduced so that everyone is clear as to who is who.

The Bride and her Parents
The bride's list is much more complicated, though the responsibility for most of the items will rest on the shoulders of her parents.

She must:

Decide (with the groom) whether to be married in church, register office or other approved premises and then complete the arrangements for the wedding service, organising the Order of Service, the music and the decorations for a service in a church and perhaps in an approved premises (other than a register office).

Select her chief bridesmaid, the bridesmaids and perhaps pages, and choose their outfits.

Make out a guest list.

Organise the reception: where to hold it, the menu and the wines.

Organise the wedding cake.

Order the flowers, bouquets, buttonholes and corsages.

Order the wedding cars to the ceremony and to the reception afterwards.

Choose the invitations, have them printed, write them and send them out.

Arrange press announcements.

Book the photographer.

Arrange for the display of the wedding presents.

She will also have to buy, hire, make or borrow:

Her wedding gown and all that goes with it (to include something old, something new, something borrowed and something blue!).

Her trousseau.

Her going away outfit.

Her luggage.

Who Pays the Bills?

Apart from the need for consultation concerning plans and arrangements, there must be some discussion concerning the payment of the bills in connection with the wedding. Everything from the decorations to the hire of the car, the wedding breakfast and the wines, the bridesmaids' dresses, the bouquets, the photographs and even the organist's fees must be met either with a cheque or in cash.

It is usual, but by no means obligatory, for the bride's parents to pay for the reception, the cake and everything concerning the celebration after the service, while the groom meets the cost of the wedding itself (clergyman's fees, organist, licence, etc.), the gifts for the bridesmaids and the honeymoon afterwards.

Naturally, the scale of the marriage and its celebration afterwards must be related to the financial status of those concerned – and where the resources of the parents differ considerably, it is usual for the better situated to pay a full measure towards the event. The cost to the bride's parents can be considerable and the bridegroom's parents should bear in mind that, generally, their own share is trivial in comparison.

Account must be taken, too, of what funds (if any) are to be held back to help the couple to start their new life together. Of course, many a bride is insistent that the wedding day is the high spot in her life, never to be repeated, and she expects it to be treated as such – and if there is anything to spare after the celebrations, maybe she wants the honeymoon to be the talking point of her memories for the rest of her life. Men are more inclined to favour less publicity and pageantry than their brides, but they are often in collusion with them concerning the scope of their honeymoon.

Other couples view the future rather differently. They realise that a large sum spent on a single day's ceremonies and jollifications plus, perhaps, a similar sum on a fortnight's honeymoon in an exotic location, might be put to more practical and permanent use. A larger down-payment on their home perhaps, less furniture on credit or HP for instance, maybe more elaborate decorations and carpeting in their new house, etc.

The Guest List
The guest list for the wedding and the reception afterwards may require careful thought. Of course the matter presents few problems where neither family has many relations or friends who could expect to be invited but in some families the numbers may well run into hundreds and even then a little forgetfulness may result in offence being taken where it was not intended.

Other couples may find that their families have a very unbalanced list of friends and relations they wish to invite to the wedding, resulting in the need for a lot of tact, common sense and maybe a certain amount of generosity.

Making bookings
All the above points need to be considered, and minds must be made up quickly if time is short before the proposed date. To get total freedom of choice, plans need to begin well in advance. Not only will there be a waiting list for available times and dates at venues for the ceremony and the reception, but almost everything else connected with a wedding is in equally urgent demand.

With holidays being booked nearly six months in advance, honeymoon reservations require equally early consideration –

and attention. The printing of invitation cards can rarely be promised under a week or two, dressmaking takes a lot of time and patience, and even the wedding cake needs care if it is to be as nice as the bride would like it to be.

The photographer will have a long list of appointments, so will the car hire firm and the florist; the caterer is likely to be booked on many dates; the hairdresser may not be available at the time required unless she is given adequate notice – and even the guests may have prior engagements!

Most of the items listed above are dealt with in subsequent chapters, but everyone involved must be aware of the amount of organisation that is going to be necessary if the wedding is to be the happy day it should be.

8

THE STAG PARTY

It has long been the custom for the prospective bridegroom to entertain his bachelor friends at a party on the night before his wedding. Traditionally, this party is viewed as the bridegroom's last 'wild fling' before he takes on the responsibilities of a married man.

But, too often, the effect on the bridegroom and the best man has been carried over to the day of the wedding. More than once in the past, because of the previous night's stag party, has a bridegroom been conducted to the wedding by his friends, hardly fit to stand alone – and certainly not sufficiently in command of his senses to be able to follow the ceremony in detail, or to make his vows in a proper spirit. The bride has found herself alone on her wedding night while her husband slept off the hangover from his stag party.

Probably with such unfortunate results in mind, it has of recent years become the practice for most prospective bridegrooms to hold their stag parties some days in advance of the wedding, instead of on the night before it, leaving time for the after-effects to wear off and for last minute arrangements for the wedding to be dealt with in an atmosphere of comparative sobriety.

A stag party is usually an informal affair, normally consisting of drinks at a local pub (or pubs). Sometimes it will include a meal. Occasionally, it will be held in a private room in a pub or in a hotel; or it may even be staged in the bridegroom's home or that of his parents (in which event the parents will, of course, be expected to go out for the evening).

It is the bridegroom's prerogative to invite only his own male friends to the stag party. As his best friend, of course, the best man will be the first to be asked (unless a female relative or friend has been invited to take on this role, in which case she should not attend this all male evening!). The others he can be expected to ask are his brothers – and, if he is wise, his bride's brothers. The actual numbers will depend on the number of friends claimed by the groom. It is generally accepted that 17 is the lower age limit, though 18 is more realistic in view of the Liquor Licensing Laws which prohibit the supplying of alcoholic beverages to anyone below that age.

Of course, the number of guests invited and the chosen entertainment – pub, club, restaurant, go-karting, etc. – will be related to the amount of money it is felt people will want to afford. It is usual for stag party guests to pay their share of the total costs and the best man should take charge of the financial details, making sure that the bill is paid (including any appropriate tip) and that he collects the shares from all the invitees. The bridegroom may decide to contribute by, for example, paying for all the pre-meal drinks (which can come to a fair sum) but if he does so the best man will make sure that all the others pay for his meal by including it in with their shares. Before deciding on any extravagant entertainment, therefore, have a thought for what the poorest guest may be able to pay and remember to warn people, in round figures, what they will be in for.

Formal invitations are quite unnecessary; a phone call or a verbal invitation when the bridegroom happens to meet his friends is sufficient. Informal dress is the norm, so the bridegroom and/or best man must make sure that everyone knows if there is any special dress requirement (perhaps ties and no trainers if a trip to a night club is planned, or sports gear, as appropriate).

The bridegroom is expected to arrive first at his party, in company with, or followed almost at once by, his best man. This allows the groom to greet his guests as they arrive while the best man dispenses, or suggests, the first round of drinks.

Of course, there will be no females among the guests and traditionally the party is restricted to unmarried men; however, most people nowadays ignore the second restriction – and as it is the bridegroom's party, who can deny him the right to stretch convention as much as he likes?

The main speech of the evening is expected to be made by the best man. If the evening includes a meal, then the best man will probably be sitting at the foot of the table and will make his speech at the coffee stage.

The speech should be entertaining, humorous, full of happy stories, and slanted to poke as much fun as possible at the bridegroom. Unless he is extremely quick-witted with an unusually fast-moving mind, the best man should prepare the text of his speech in advance and, if necessary, rehearse it to the point where it sounds 'off the cuff' and unrehearsed.

The contents must be amusing, anecdotal and entirely concerned with the bridegroom and his friends. However, it should not be too long or the listeners will get bored.

The best man may make use of his personal knowledge of the groom and refer to:

An event or two which took place during their schooldays;

The unfortunate girls – unnamed – that are now to be abandoned by the bridegroom . . . and the difficulties in getting rid of them;

The idea that two can live as cheaply as one being a fallacy;

Some of the means whereby he can escape his fate: the river, the French Foreign Legion, a Trappist Monastery or a slow boat to the East.

The bridegroom responds with an equally farcical farewell to his 'bachelor' friends – friends whom he is glad to abandon because of their shockingly selfish way of life; a bunch of reprobates, boozers and ill-mannered oafs.

The bridegroom can include in his speech, humorously:

A sad farewell to his past girlfriends.

A welcome at his home for all his male friends – so long as they wipe their shoes on the doormat.

A request that financial aid should not be withheld if they ever again meet in a pub.

An entertainment is not really necessary at such a party. However, if there is one it should be confined to a single act, e.g. a comedian. A female entertainer may be engaged, *but only* if the bride is not likely to be upset to hear about it.

The bridegroom should be the last to leave the party – usually in company with his best man and, if necessary, by taxi. The best man should be in a fit state to make sure that anyone driving home from the party is fully sober.

9

THE HEN PARTY

Not to be out-done, the bride often organises her own celebration with her chief bridesmaid, sisters (both hers and the groom's, if appropriate) and female friends. (The bridesmaids may be included, too, if they are not too young.) This is often a quieter event than the groom's Stag Party – although not always!

The way in which a Hen Party is celebrated is entirely up to the bride. For example, many choose to go to a pub and/or club, others arrange a meal in a restaurant or at home, while yet others may opt for an evening (or perhaps a day) at a health club for a spot of pampering.

Invitation is usually by word of mouth and it should be made clear to anyone invited what the plan for the evening is, so they can dress appropriately and know what the likely cost is to be. A thought should be spared for the poorest in the group during the organising of the evening and nothing planned that will over-stretch such pockets.

A sensible bride will organise her Hen Party to take place well before her wedding. Last minute arrangements may well take up most of her time on the day before the wedding, so she'll need to be clear-headed for them, and on the evening before her big day she will want to be able to take a break from all the bustle of preparation and have time to relax (as much as she can!).

10

WHO DOES WHAT?

One of the earliest tasks of the bride and the bridegroom is to choose who are to be their helpers before, during and immediately after their wedding.

The matter needs careful thought if jealousies are not to be aroused. Relations often feel that they have a claim to be more than guests at a wedding; long-standing friends expect similar privileges – and not one of them may be suited to the particular duties involved.

Possibly he who considers himself most entitled to the office of best man is debarred because he has too little time to spare before the wedding, perhaps because he knows so few of the people concerned and would, in consequence, make a poor marshal, and not improbably because, however sincere he may be, he may lack the flair for organisation, the capacity to take charge of a situation, or not be quick-witted enough to deal with an emergency.

Equally, an 'anxious-to-be' bridesmaid may not be led to understand that she is the 'one-too-many' of the girls who can hope to be invited to join the bridal procession. Maybe, too, her lack of composure would be likely to cause embarrassment during the ceremony, or possibly she has been excluded because her ability to remain standing on her feet throughout the service is in doubt – or even because her height just cannot be matched to that of any other suitable girl.

Others, of course, have duties which are inescapable. The need for the bride's father to be present at the church to give her away, for instance, is almost obligatory. Only where he is dead, physically incapable of attending the service or estranged from the family should a deputy be appointed.

The Chief Bridesmaid
It is quite usual for the bride to seek the help of her eldest
unmarried sister as her chief bridesmaid, or, if she has no sister,
another unmarried relative or her best unmarried friend.

There is no bounden duty laid on the bride to make such a
choice if she considers another unmarried relative or friend
temperamentally more suitable – but the alternative selection
should not be made lightly and the unmarried sister or best friend
who has been passed over should be told by the bride herself the
reason for her decision, in the hope that goodwill and harmony
will not be jeopardized.

The chief bridesmaid's duties are concerned mainly with two
things: personal attention to the bride, and the marshalling of the
bridesmaids and pages.

She might be expected to help the bride to choose the bridesmaids' dresses, to rehearse them in their duties and to take charge
of the bride's bouquet during the service.

She might be called upon to help dress the bride for her
wedding, though this task is usually claimed by the bride's
mother as a last service to her daughter. In any event, the chief
bridesmaid will have enough to do to dress herself and to see to it
that the bridesmaids are properly dressed for the occasion; their
head-dresses, their posies, their shoes and the correct hang of
their dresses – not to mention their arrival at the church well in
advance of the bride.

During the service, the chief bridesmaid's station is immediately behind the bride and the bride's father. She will follow them
in procession to the chancel steps or to the registrar and then,
passing her own bouquet to the nearest bridesmaid, she will take
the bridal bouquet and draw the bride's veil clear of her face.

If the service is held in a church, when the newly-wed couple
follow the clergyman into the vestry for the formality of signing
the register, she and the best man follow immediately behind
them.

Often the chief bridesmaid (if she is of age) and the best man
are chosen to sign the register as witnesses to the marriage.

The chief bridesmaid should be available to the bride during
the reception, to smooth away any little worries or difficulties

that may arise – often in consultation with the best man. Her final duty is to help the bride into her 'going away' outfit if she is needed, and to see her to the car.

The Bridesmaids
The bridesmaids are chosen by the bride from amongst her young friends and relatives or those of the bridegroom. They generally number two or four, though for high-profile weddings the numbers may rise as high as six or even eight. The bride's attendants need not all be girls; young boys may be included as pages. Pages are always very young – 5 to 8 years of age are the most acceptable limits, although there is nothing mandatory about it. They are nearly always young brothers or nephews of the couple.

It is worth remembering that while very small bridesmaids and pages may look adorable, they are going to find standing still without talking during the service very difficult, and it is common sense to choose children of an age that can understand what is required and what is going on.

A bride almost always tries to match the bridesmaids and pages for size, sometimes a difficult task but making a most attractive picture when she has been successful. It is the bride's prerogative, too, to choose the material and pattern for the bridesmaids' dresses and the pages' outfits, and any accessories to be worn and bouquets etc. to be carried.

By tradition, the mothers of the bridesmaids each pay for their daughter's attire – an expensive business if the bride's choice happens to be ambitious. Hopefully they will be used as party dresses afterwards.

The bride should take care not to invite anyone to act as her bridesmaid whose parents would be unlikely to welcome the expense – unless, as is sometimes the case, the bride's parents will provide the whole of the ensemble for each of the brides-maids. Whoever pays for the dresses and accessories, it is usual to allow the bridesmaids to keep them after the wedding unless they are hired.

Most large department stores have a bridal department where there is a wide range of bridal gowns, veils, head dresses and bridesmaids' dresses to choose from. Alternatively, a good dressmaker could prove of immense help in deciding on the ensemble; she will advise, too, on what is suitable for the time of the year, the fashionable styles, and have a sense of matching colours and of trimmings that will enhance the group as a whole. She will be able to make suggestions concerning the modern trend in head-dresses, be that hats, tiaras, circlets or bows. She will know whether or not a veil should be worn by the bride and even be able to advise on the most suitable posies or flower baskets to match or contrast with the dresses. There are also plenty of bridal magazines on the market which are full of current trends and ideas.

The duty of the bridesmaids and pages is to assist the bride from the moment she arrives at the venue for her wedding until she finally leaves the reception on the first stage of her honeymoon. 'Assist' is hardly the word as far as the wedding ceremony is concerned; the bridesmaids and pages are merely decorative in the procession and have no duty other than to attend to the bridal train – if it should be long enough to require attention. In the procession they follow in pairs behind the bride, the pages leading and the taller or older bridesmaids coming last.

At the reception afterwards, the bridesmaids might be expected to take round portions of the wedding cake, at the proper time, and offer them to the guests – but after that their duties are complete and they can enjoy themselves for the rest of the day as each of them sees fit.

Matron of Honour

There is no absolute need for a bride to be attended by a retinue of bridesmaids. Sometimes it may be that she has no young female relatives or, indeed, any suitable young friends available. This often happens if the bride is new to the district, or has travelled some considerable distance to marry.

Sometimes, too, the bride may be older and young bridesmaids may be out of place; or it may even be that she is most anxious to ask some particular woman to attend her who happens to be married, especially a sister.

In all such cases it is quite usual for the bride to be attended by a matron of honour. The lady chosen will be a married woman and she will be the only attendant, acting as the chief – and only – bridesmaid.

Her duties are identical with those of a chief bridesmaid, but she will not wear the finery. The bride, too, usually abandons the full wedding dress and veil for an outfit similar to that worn by her matron of honour – though this is by no means a must.

The Bride's Mother

The bride's mother is one of those who have inescapable duties to perform in connection with her daughter's wedding – unless she happens to be incapacitated, when her mantle will fall on the bride's oldest sister if she has one, or an aunt or even a grandmother.

Yet, despite the fact that she will probably have to work harder than anyone else to make for the success of the occasion, the bride's mother will have almost no official part in the wedding itself.

She will carry the whole of the responsibility for the social side of the event and as the hostess she will issue the invitations to the wedding guests both to the ceremony and to the reception afterwards. She will need to exercise a great deal of tact, too, to include as far as possible the guests suggested by the bride-groom's parents, bearing in mind that she and her husband will be expected to pay the bills!

The bride's mother will be deeply concerned in helping to choose the bridal gown and no doubt her advice will be sought concerning the bridesmaid's dresses.

Among the other cares she must shoulder, in consultation with the bride, are:

1. The choosing, printing and despatching of the invitations.
2. The press announcements.
3. The printing of the Order of Service as arranged between the couple and the clergyman or registrar.
4. The decorations for the venue of the ceremony.
5. The wedding bouquets, buttonholes and corsages for the two mothers – in consultation with the bride to make sure that they are all in harmony.

6. Ordering the wedding cars to take the bride and her father, the bridesmaids, and of course herself, to the ceremony. She may also need to order cars wanted by other guests – and to make arrangements to get everybody from the ceremony to the reception afterwards. The only cars that will not require her attention are those that will carry the bridegroom and his best man to the ceremony and the 'going away' car for the bridal couple on the first stage of their honeymoon, which the bridegroom should arrange.

7. She will have to make and ice (or have made and iced) the wedding cake and arrange for its delivery to the reception venue.

8. The photographer needs to be booked. He will normally take photographs of the bride arriving with her father for the ceremony and may, if asked, go to the bride's house before the wedding party depart for the ceremony to take a few photographs there. Sometimes he is allowed to take photographs during parts of the service or during the signing of the register, but most photographs will be of the bride and groom with their bridesmaids and pages, their parents and other relatives after the ceremony is finished. The photographer will, if the couple wish, take some black and white shots and, together with a form which includes all the relevant details and will have been completed by the bride and groom, send one to the local newspaper who will print it free of charge at the editor's discretion. The photographer will also arrive at the reception before the guests to take the 'official' and 'pretend' photograph of the cutting of the cake. The cake usually has several tiers and this may be the only time to photograph it complete, as many caterers take away the middle tier to cut it up during the reception. There will be plenty of amateur photographers around to capture the actual moment of the cutting of the cake.

9. Arranging for a video recording to be taken of the ceremony, and perhaps the celebrations afterwards, with the approval of the clergyman or registrar conducting the ceremony.

10. Arranging the details of the reception in consultation with the caterer and arranging where this is to be held, including:

(a) the menu
(b) the wines
(c) the table decorations
(d) the seating arrangements
(e) booking a private room for the bride where she can change into her 'going away' outfit
(f) drawing up a table plan if needed
(g) arranging the printing of place cards, menus, book matches, table napkins, as desired.
11. The collection of what is left of the wedding cake after the reception; the cutting and boxing of the portions for posting to distant relatives and friends.

(There are some firms who will take on everything for the bride's mother, from catering to car hire, flowers, photography, video recording, the wedding cake, entertainment, stationery, bridal wear and hire facilities.)

As the wedding will, in all probability, take place in the district of the bride's family home, her mother can expect to do some entertaining in addition to the gathering of friends and relatives at the reception. This will be particularly strenuous if the bride-groom, his family and friends come from any considerable distance.

As the hostess, the bride's mother may find herself involved in arranging hotel accommodation for some of the guests and may even feel duty bound to put some of the bridegroom's relatives up in her own home. She should be aware, however, that on the day of the wedding itself it may cause difficulties if there are too many people in the house. It should be remembered that the bridesmaids will be meeting there to get ready for the wedding, the photographer may well come round before the wedding to take pictures of the bride at home and there will be bustle enough without the addition of overnight guests.

She will also find that her daughter will need her help in dressing for the wedding. Although it is the duty of the chief bridesmaid to attend the bride, few mothers are willing to forego this last chore for their daughters. She will then leave the bride at home with her father and make haste, either alone or with the bridesmaids, to reach the church or civil venue ahead of her.

Her place during the marriage service is in the front row of the pews on the bride's side of the aisle, to the left facing the altar for a church wedding, or the front seats in a civil ceremony, among her other children and perhaps her parents.

She takes no part in the ceremony, although if it is a church wedding she will be led by the bridegroom's father to the vestry (perhaps as a witness to the signing of the marriage register). She comes out of the church on the left arm of the bridegroom's father following the pages and bridesmaids in procession, with the bridegroom's mother and the bride's father behind them.

She and her husband should leave for the reception immediately after the newly-weds. They are the hosts and must, of course, be there first, in time to receive their guests.

The Bride's Father

The bride's father has the dual privilege of giving his daughter away at her wedding – and paying for the reception afterwards.

Attired in morning dress or lounge suit (to match the rest of the men in the wedding party), and wearing a buttonhole similar to that worn by the bridegroom and the best man, the bride's father escorts his daughter from their home to the ceremony. If for any reason her father is unable to attend the wedding, the bride's eldest brother, uncle or male guardian usually takes his place (although, of course, there is no reason why her mother cannot give her away, if the bride so desires – and the mother agrees).

He arrives at the venue for the ceremony with the bride after everyone else has gathered within, though it is bad form to keep everyone waiting after the appointed time. Almost at once, with his daughter on his right arm, he will lead the procession towards the chancel steps or other agreed place, as appropriate (depending on whether the ceremony is to take place in a church or in a building registered for civil marriages). At a register office the guests will often be waiting outside and the wedding party all enter the building together.

At the proper time in the church service, he will take his daughter's hand and give it to the clergyman in a gesture of giving her away. (This is not a part of the civil ceremony.) After the service, the bride's father accompanies the bridegroom's mother into the vestry in the wake of the newly-weds, to see the final act of the marriage – the signing of the register.

Immediately after leaving the ceremony he will hurry with his wife to the venue of the reception where, as host and hostess, they greet their guests.

Finally, the bride's father will be called on by the best man, during the reception, to propose the toast of the 'Bride and Bridegroom'.

The Best Man
The best man is chosen by the bridegroom from amongst his relatives or friends. He is traditionally unmarried, although, in general, it is the groom's closest companion that is honoured. (He might also, in very rare circumstances, be a she – see page 51.)

The duties are onerous and the bridegroom would be well advised to make his selection with extreme care. The best man will find himself a sort of master of ceremonies, the chief usher, the repository of valuables – such as the wedding ring(s) and the certificate permitting the marriage – organiser-in-chief, toastmaster and paymaster. He is also likely to find himself the bridegroom's messenger boy, father confessor, persuader, remembrance, office boy and valet.

Obviously he must have a flair for organisation, a steady nerve, be a good mixer and have limitless tact. His many duties include:

1. Getting the bridegroom to his wedding – on time. (He should talk to the groom in advance of the day to establish the arrangements for getting himself and the groom to the ceremony.)
2. Detailing the ushers to their duties.
3. Safeguarding the wedding ring(s) until exchanged by the couple.
4. After the service, accompanying the chief bridesmaid to the vestry, if appropriate, behind the bride and bridegroom.
5. Possibly to act as a witness to the signing of the register, often with the chief bridesmaid. (The bride and groom may,

of course, choose other witnesses and, to avoid confusion at the very last moment, it is well that it be decided and confirmed who the official witnesses are to be well in advance.)

6. He should follow the bride and groom out of the ceremony with the chief bridesmaid and then be at the door to usher the newly-weds to their places in front of the photographer and see them to their car for the journey to the reception. He then ushers the guests into their cars in turn – parents first, grandparents, uncles and aunts, bridesmaids and then the friends and more distant relatives.

7. He pays the marriage fees as appropriate (possibly including the cost of the organist, the choir and bells) if this has not already been done.

8. At the reception he calls on the speakers and replies to the toast of 'The Bridesmaids' on their behalf.

9. He reads out any messages of congratulations that have been received.

10. He sees the couple into their car or taxi after the reception (which he may have to organise – another detail to check well in advance of the wedding day), ready for the start of their honeymoon journey, hands over the various documents such as rail or air tickets, passports, traveller's cheques, route maps and perhaps luggage which he may have been safe-guarding during the ceremony and the reception.

Though the best man is traditionally supposed to help the bride-groom to dress for his wedding, this is hardly necessary with modern clothes. In the picturesque days of the Prince Regent, of course, with the magnificent velvets, silks and satins, socks, stockings and shoe buckles worn by the bridegrooms, the best man needed the services of a valet to help him dress the nervous buck – and many an hour to spare for the purpose!

Today, the best man usually arrives at the bridegroom's home as the latter is dressing, collects the wedding ring(s), identifies the baggage, takes charge of the keys, the various tickets and other documents needed for the honeymoon and the cash neces-sary to pay any outstanding marriage fees – in other words, generally checks that nothing has been forgotten. Even then he will probably find that the nervous bridegroom has neglected to provide himself with a pair of black socks or has broken a shoelace and there isn't a spare!

Once he and the bridegroom are ready there is nothing for it but to watch the clock and worry about getting to the ceremony in good time. Nothing could make a more embarrassing start to a wedding than for the bridegroom to arrive at the ceremony after his bride! From then on he continually fingers the ring(s) in his waistcoat pocket, knowing that though he would be by no means the first best man to forget it, his failure to produce it at the right moment might constitute a disaster.

The best man's clothes are similar to those worn by the bridegroom. If it is a very formal wedding and the groom is wearing morning dress, then the best man would wear the same. For less formal weddings the groom and best man wear lounge suits, often matching ones. (The female best man should also be readily identifiable in her role and a formal skirt suit with a buttonhole to match that of the groom would be most appropriate.)

Whatever the type of wedding, the bridegroom and best man wear buttonholes, which the best man should collect unless they are being delivered straight to the groom's house. It is usual for the groom and best man and the two fathers to have the same buttonholes – white, red, pink or yellow carnations or roses – while the ushers all have white or red buttonholes. But it is equally possible for the groom to have a buttonhole to harmonise with his suit. The choice is usually the bride's who will order all the flowers with her mother.

Ushers or 'Groomsmen'

When appointing ushers, the bridegroom (generally in consultation with his best man and often the bride) must take into account family 'considerations'. It is usual to make the choice from the unmarried brothers and friends of both the bridegroom and his bride, and a great deal of tact needs to be exercised if somebody is not going to protest: 'If you ask *him* you can't leave out *so-and-so*'. It is important that each side should be represented in order that as many of the guests as possible will be recognised and received by name.

The number of ushers required will depend largely on the number of people who are invited to the ceremony. If less than fifty or sixty guests are invited, then only two ushers are generally needed. A further two ushers could well be needed to cope with each additional fifty/sixty guests, though there is no hard and fast ruling on the matter. The need is to have sufficient ushers to receive the guests, hand them Order of Service sheets (if appropriate) and conduct them to their places for the ceremony.

The ushers must, of course, arrive first at the venue for the ceremony to greet the guests as they appear. It is quite correct for an usher to meet a guest in the entrance and ask 'Friend of the bride, or of the groom?', in order to determine on which side they should sit, but it is much more welcoming to receive them by name and, thus, know to which side they should be conducted. Tradition dictates that relatives and friends of the bride sit on the left of the aisle facing the chancel steps or the place where the ceremony will take place, and those of the bridegroom on the right – the immediate families of the bride and bridegroom being placed in the front rows on their respective sides. This system would work just as well at a civil venue if it is possible to organise the seating in this way (although register offices are often limited in space).

Dress for the ushers should be similar to that worn by the bridegroom and best man: morning dress or dark lounge suits. Buttonholes, usually of carnations, are worn in their coat lapels.

During the ceremony the ushers should sit near the back in order to be in a convenient position to deal with any late-comers and to open the doors for the bridal party to process out, if appropriate.

Chief usher
If the best man lives far from the bridegroom or, because of circumstances, is able to travel to the venue of the wedding and stay there for just a few days (or perhaps only the day of the wedding itself) it may be advisable to appoint a chief usher or 'deputy best man'.

The choice of such an individual should be made by consultation between the bridegroom and the best man, bearing in mind that:

(a) he must be willing, capable and have the time to act as deputy to the best man during probably the whole of the preliminaries;

(b) he must be a friend of the bridegroom as they will be involved together making the arrangements and carrying out the practical details;

(c) he must be a close friend of the best man who will expect him to have ready, and be able to turn over to him with the shortest of briefings, all the information and items he will require for the wedding.

The duties of chief usher are, of course, those of the best man, up to and until the best man is available to take over for himself.

However, in his role as usher his most important duty is to take responsibility for greeting the mother of the bride when she arrives and conduct her to the front left-hand pew or row of seats.

11

ANNOUNCEMENTS

The first public proclamation of the forthcoming wedding is made at the time of the engagement of the couple. Such announcements receive much less attention than they did some years ago, and, in fact, there is no longer any absolute need to have the event published in the press at all.

However, there are occasions when an announcement in the advertisement columns of the press is of value to the newly engaged couple – particularly to those who have a very wide circle of friends and acquaintances. In such instances it might well be impractical to write a letter to every one of them.

Sometimes, too, it might be that one or other of the couple (or one of their parents) happens to be a figure of national importance or of wide public interest – a politician or a pop singer perhaps – making the announcement a matter of public interest. Any such announcements, of course, would be enough to bring the reporters and photographers flocking to the door!

In such cases, and where friends and relatives of the couple are widely scattered over the country, the announcements should be made in one or more of the national daily newspapers where a wide circulation is assured. *The Times, The Daily Telegraph, The Guardian* and *The Independent* are four which spring to mind at once as publishing special announcement columns.

If it happens, however, that the friends and relatives are fairly tightly domiciled in a single large city or county, the local newspaper is a better medium in which to advertise than the national morning newspapers and is, of course, considerably less expensive. If the bride and bridegroom do happen to live in districts distant from one another, it might be wise to use the press of each locality in which to announce the engagement and the forthcoming wedding.

The advertisement should be sent to the Classified Advertisements Manager of the newspaper(s) concerned, and should be drafted in the following manner to appear under 'Forthcoming Marriages'.

Mr P J Fry and Miss A Lloyd

The engagement is announced between Peter John Fry, only son of Mr and Mrs G H Fry of Esher, Surrey, and Ann, youngest daughter of Col and Mrs L R Lloyd of Horsham, West Sussex.

It could be varied to read:

The marriage has been arranged and will take place shortly between Peter, only son of Mr and Mrs G H Fry of Esher, Surrey, and Ann, youngest daughter of Col and Mrs L R Lloyd of Horsham, West Sussex.

If, however, the bridegroom has a title or carries a military rank, the wording to the announcement would more probably be as follows:

Flight Lieut P J Fry and Miss A Lloyd

The engagement is announced between Flight Lieutenant Peter John Fry, AFC, RAF, only son of Mr and Mrs G H Fry of Esher, Surrey, and Ann, youngest daughter of Col and Mrs L R Lloyd of Horsham, West Sussex.

Many people use their local newspaper to announce engagements and these normally appear under 'Births, Marriages and Deaths' columns. They tend to be less formal and would read as follows:

LLOYD-FRY – Mr and Mrs Robert Lloyd of Horsham are pleased to announce the engagement of their youngest daughter, Ann, to Peter, only son of Mr and Mrs G H Fry of Esher, Surrey.

And for the groom's local paper:

FRY-LLOYD – Mr and Mrs G H Fry of Esher are pleased to announce the engagement of their only son, Peter, to Ann, youngest daughter of Mr and Mrs Robert Lloyd of Horsham, West Sussex.

If it should be that the bride's father is dead, the second part of the announcement should read:

. . . and Ann, youngest daughter of Mrs Lloyd and the late Col L R Lloyd of Horsham, West Sussex.

If it is the bride's mother who has died, the sentence will read:

. . . and Ann, the youngest daughter of Col L R Lloyd and the late Mrs Lloyd of Horsham, West Sussex.

If the bride's parents have been divorced, the address of each of them should be given, as follows:

. . . and Ann, youngest daughter of Col L R Lloyd of Horsham, West Sussex, and Mrs R L Lloyd of Guildford, Surrey.

If the parents have been divorced and the bride's mother has re-married, the announcement should conclude:

. . . and Ann, youngest daughter of Col L R Lloyd of Horsham, West Sussex, and Mrs C B Brooklyn of Coldharbour, Surrey.

If it is the bridegroom's parents who are either dead or have been divorced, precisely the same amendment should be made to the first part of the announcement as would be made to the second part of the sentence where the bride is concerned.

The day after the wedding a press announcement can appear under the 'Marriages' column. The most usual wording is as follows:

Mr P J Green and Miss A White

The marriage took place on 20th April at the Church of St George, Woodhouse, of Mr Peter J Green, only son of Mr and Mrs A F Green of Esher, Surrey, and Miss Ann White, eldest daughter of Mr and Mrs J F White of Tonbridge, Kent.

Where one party has been divorced the wording could be:

Mr P J Green and Miss A White

A service of blessing was held yesterday at the Church of St Mark, Balham, after the marriage of Mr Peter Green, only son of Mr and Mrs A F Green of Esher, Surrey, and Miss Ann White, eldest daughter of Mr and Mrs F J White of Tonbridge, Kent. The Rev J M Graham officiated.

Or the wording can be simpler:

Mr P J Green and Miss A White

The marriage took place quietly in Baldock on 20th April between Mr Peter J Green and Miss Ann White.

Local papers are often weekly and any marriage announcements sent to such papers should be worded to reflect this.

12

SENDING OUT THE INVITATIONS

In due course invitations to the wedding and the reception need to be printed and despatched by post to those for whom they are intended. The list is a matter for the bride's parents (assuming they are the hosts), as they must select their guests. But it is common and much kinder for the two sets of parents and the engaged couple to consult one another on the subject.

It is reasonable to assume that both the bride and the bridegroom – and their parents – will wish to invite similar numbers from amongst their own relatives and friends, though this is not necessarily the case. For instance, a bridegroom may come from some considerable distance to his wedding; a distance not easily covered by all his friends. Or perhaps the bride is a member of some society which might bring her an unusually large number of friends.

In any event, the bride's parents (as hosts) must be left to make the final decision as to numbers to be invited – at least as far as the reception is concerned; they will be expected to pay the bill for the whole of the entertainment and it could well be an embarrassing amount, although it is becoming more common for both families to share the cost and even for the bride and bridegroom to make a contribution.

Invitations should be sent out well in advance of the event; at least six weeks before the wedding, preferably earlier, so as to give the guests plenty of time to complete their own arrangements and to decline any alternative invitations they may receive to other functions on the same day at the same time. (If anyone among the proposed guest list is a particularly busy person, or the

wedding is booked for a busy holiday period, it may be as well to
let him or her know the date as soon as it has been fixed in order
to avoid the disappointment of some favourite relative or friend
being unable to attend.)

The invitations can be printed in a standard fashion, leaving the
sender to fill in names in the appropriate places. Any good
stationers or printers will have a wide range of wedding stationery
available from which a choice can be made. These include
invitations (perhaps with a tear off reply slip); Order of Service
sheets; menu cards; place cards; serviettes and rings; book
matches; ashtrays and drip mats with the bride and groom's
Christian names and the wedding date. The stationers may also
provide the boxes and cards for sending wedding cake to those
unable to attend.

A very popular format for the invitation is:

> *Colonel and Mrs Leslie R White*
> *request the pleasure of the company of*
> ....
> *at the marriage of their daughter*
> *Ann*
> *with*
> *Mr Peter John Green*
> *at St George's Parish Church, Ashford*
> *on Saturday, 20th April [date]*
> *at 11 am*
> *and at a reception afterwards at the*
> *Carlton Hotel.*

12 Fir Tree Lane
Ashford
Kent   *RSVP*

The RSVP is essential because the hostess must know in advance
how many guests she may expect – especially for the meal at the
reception.

Of course, the wording of the first part of the invitation will vary with the status of those sending out the invitations. If either of the bride's parents is dead, the name of the surviving parent is sufficient

Colonel Leslie R White
requests the pleasure . . .

or

Mrs Joan R White
requests the pleasure . . .

or the order of the wording could be changed to leave the space for the invitee's name at the top followed by

The pleasure of your company
is requested at the marriage of
Ann
daughter of Col Leslie R White and
the late Mrs Joan White . . .

If the bride's parents are divorced and the wife has re-married or reverted to her maiden name, the invitation should read:

Colonel Leslie R White and Mrs Joan Bodkin
request the pleasure . . .

or, if the wife has not re-married, the following wording may be preferred:

Colonel Leslie R White and Joan White
request the pleasure . . .

Invitations to a register office wedding are similar and would read:

Mr and Mrs A B Cox
request the pleasure of the company of
....
at the marriage of their daughter
Jane
with
Mr James Brown
at the Register Office, Park Road
on Thursday, 10th May [date]
at 11.30 am
and at a reception afterwards at the
Royal Hotel.

12 Dorset Street
Weymouth
Dorset   *RSVP*

If both parents are dead, the invitations will be issued in the names of the guardians or relatives who are to act as hosts for the occasion, or if the couple are sending the invitations themselves they would, obviously, have their names printed at the top:

Peter Fry and Ann Lloyd
request the pleasure of the company of
....
at their marriage at

Whilst it is usual to combine an invitation to the wedding ceremony and the reception afterwards it is also possible to issue separate invitations. It may be that the couple would prefer a private, family wedding or that the church or register office will only hold a certain number of people. Alternatively, it may be that numbers have to be limited for the wedding breakfast but more people could be invited to an evening reception afterwards. In all variations the wording of the invitation must be completely clear so that the invitees all understand where they are expected and when.

Where the wedding service is a small, family affair and a

reception is to be held to include other guests who were not at the ceremony the invitation would read:

Mr and Mrs J S White
request the pleasure of the company of
....
on the evening of the wedding
of their daughter
Maria
with
Mr Peter J Green
at The Park Hotel, Kings Road
at 7.30 pm
on Friday, 7th May [date]

12 Fir Tree Lane
Woodhouse   *RSVP*

An alternative form is:

Mr and Mrs J S White
request the pleasure of the company of
....
at an evening reception
at The Royal Hotel, The Mall
at 7 pm
to celebrate the marriage of their daughter
Susan
with
Mr George Black
on Saturday 30th April [year]

12 Fir Tree Lane
Woodhouse   *RSVP*

It is also possible that if the reception is to take place over the course of an afternoon and evening, with larger numbers attending in the evening, the couple may wish to invite the evening guests to the ceremony itself (especially if it is taking place in a large church). This is quite acceptable and a possible wording for such an invitation is as follows:

Mr and Mrs A B Cox
request the pleasure of the company of
....
at the marriage of their daughter
Jane
with
Mr James Brown
at St Mark's Church, Park Road, Anytown
on Thursday, 10th May [date]
at 11.30 am
and at an evening reception from 7 pm
at the Royal Hotel.

12 Dorset Street
Weymouth
Dorset   *RSVP*

The subject of whether or not to invite children to a wedding is often a fraught one. Many brides do not want their day spoiled by crying or over-excited children and the hosts may object to the additional cost of young guests who neither chose nor wished to attend. Whatever the decision, where a family is being invited it is important to make clear exactly who the invitation applies to. If children are included, their names should be listed; if they are not, the names of the parents only should be listed. Tact and diplomacy may be required but it is the right of the hosts to make the decision and guests should respect that.

If there are to be a number of children at the wedding it could be worth organising a crêche to be run during the service so that the problem of bored children does not occur. This would only be possible where there is a convenient room within or near to the place where the ceremony is taking place and it should be staffed by responsible adults, preferably with plenty of experience in looking after children. Some of the parents may wish to stay with their children, but many will welcome the opportunity to enjoy the wedding without distraction. Don't forget to let guests know that their children should be left at the crêche and send out full instructions as to its location with the invitation.

13

REPLIES TO INVITATIONS

Replies to wedding invitations should be brief and should be despatched without delay. There are many pre-printed reply cards available nowadays which leave a space for the invitee to write their name(s) and if these are not used any written reply should be couched in the third person, such as:

15 Winsgrove Terrace
Ellesmere

Mr and Mrs Joseph Fleet and their daughter, Phyllis, thank Colonel and Mrs Leslie R White for their kind invitation to their daughter's wedding at St George's Parish Church on Saturday 20th April [date] at 11 am and to a reception afterwards at the Carlton Hotel, and are most happy to accept.

11th March [date]

Such a note requires no signature.

It is important that the name of every person planning to attend the wedding is included on the reply. This allows the host to correct any misunderstanding that may have arisen and to ensure that an accurate note of the numbers attending can be kept.

If it is impossible to accept the invitation, either because of a prior engagement or for some private family reason, it is a matter of courtesy both to acknowledge the invitation, and to make the decision not to attend clear. The names of all those unable to attend should be listed.

Again, there are many pre-printed cards available but if the refusal is to be hand written it should be as brief as the acceptance and similarly written in the third person, though an excuse might be added, however vague it may appear to be:

15 Winsgrove Terrace
Ellesmere

Mr and Mrs Joseph Fleet and their daughter, Phyllis, thank Colonel and Mrs Leslie R White for their kind invitation to their daughter's wedding at St George's Parish Church on Saturday 20th April [date] and to the reception afterwards.
 Unfortunately they have accepted a prior engagement for that date and must therefore decline with regret.

11th March [date]

Again, no signature is required.

Sometimes invitations already accepted must later be declined, possibly because of illness, an accident, or even through a sudden death in the family. In such a case the hosts should be informed at once. It may give them time to amend the numbers given to the caterers. A telephone call should be made to the hosts as soon as possible but also a simple note may be appreciated by the hostess, which should make clear who cannot attend if only one of the invited party is affected. Perhaps:

15 Winsgrove Terrace
Ellesmere

Mrs Joseph Fleet sincerely regrets the necessity, due to illness, to have to inform you that she will now be unable to attend your daughter's wedding on 20th April [date] or the reception afterwards.
 Mr Joseph Fleet and his daughter, Phyllis, will, however, still be delighted to attend.

14th April [date]

Again, there is no need for a signature.

Where children are invited the hosts should make this clear on the invitations sent out. If there is any doubt, however, the hosts should be politely asked for clarification. There should be no offence taken if the children are not included – wedding receptions are extremely expensive things to put on and limits have to be set somewhere. Remember that what adults see as a day of celebration and excitement is seen by most children as boring and would test the patience of even the best behaved. If children are invited, parents should be sensitive to the fact that the ceremony itself is a special moment not only for the bride and groom but also for many of the guests. Noisy children will be an unwelcome distraction and sensible parents will agree before the ceremony begins whether one will stay outside with the children or be ready to take them out if they become a nuisance. The same applies when the speeches are being made at the reception.

Presents
There is a certain amount of tradition to be observed in the sending of wedding presents:

(a) Relatives should send a present whether or not they attend the reception and the wedding – so long as they have been invited.

(b) All those attending the wedding ceremony and the reception afterwards are expected to send a present.

(c) There is no need for a friend to send a present when the invitation has been declined – though it is usual to do so when the cause is illness or some other reason that, if it had not arisen, would not have meant a refusal.

(d) There is no need to send a present where the invitation is to the wedding ceremony only – and does not include the reception afterwards.

(e) All presents sent before the wedding should be sent to the bride at her parents' home. If they are sent afterwards, they should be addressed to both the bride and bridegroom at their new home.

(f) If a present is received, it is good manners to invite the giver to the wedding ceremony and usually, though not necessarily, to the reception afterwards. To avoid any embarrassment on this score it is best to wait until invitations to the wedding and the reception have been received before sending presents.

14

WEDDING GIFTS

Traditionally wedding gifts are sent to the bride at her home (even if the donor is a friend of the groom who has never met the bride). These days, however, many guests take their presents to the reception. The presents may vary from the decorative to the practical, from the purely personal to the 'homey' and from the very expensive to the intrinsically valueless.

Most couples will spend some time compiling a gift list so that when friends telephone to find out what the couple would like as a wedding present they can be given several ideas or even sent a copy of the list. Some couples may feel awkward about doing this but most guests will welcome the opportunity to purchase a gift that the couple really want.

If a list is to be made out it should be specific – giving the product, the manufacturer, the style, colour, etc., and where it can be obtained. A full range of prices should be covered, to give freedom of choice to all the guests. The following outline list is just a guide:

Living Room	Bedroom	Bathroom
Clock	Pillows	Towels
Cushions	Duvet	Bath mat
Nest of tables	Sheets	Mirror
Lamps	Duvet covers	Linen basket
Music centre	Blankets	Bath rack
Television set	Pillow cases	Indoor clothes line
Video player	Bedspread	Bathroom scales
Vases	Bedside clock/	Towel rail
Chairs	tea maker	Soap holder

Settee

Rugs

Electric blanket

Long mirror

Shower curtain

Kitchen

Refrigerator/
  freezer

Washing machine

Dishwasher

Cooker

Food mixer

Electric kettle

Coffee percolator

Kitchen knives

Bread board

Toaster

Slow cooker

Microwave oven

Sandwich maker

Mixing bowls

Saucepans

Tea towels

Can opener

Kitchen scales

Pressure cooker

Storage jars

Trays

Wooden spoons

Pedal bin

Washing up bowl

Casserole set

Frying pan

Oven gloves

Spice rack

Dining Room

Dining table
  & chairs

Place mats

Tablecloths

Hostess trolley

Dinner service*

Tea service*

Breakfast set

Salt/pepper mills

Fruit bowl

Cutlery

Water jug

Tumblers

Wine glasses

Sherry glasses

Decanters

Sideboard

Cheese board &
  knife

Hot plate

Candlesticks

Clock

Miscellaneous

Vacuum cleaner

Brushes & mops

Dustpan & brush

Garden furniture

Garden tools

Garden tubs

Shrubs & trees

Lawn mower

Car rug

Picnic set

Ornaments

Wine rack

Wastepaper baskets

Luggage

(*These expensive items could be listed in small lots to make parts that are more generally affordable, i.e. 4 side plates, 4 dinner plates, 4 cups and saucers, etc.)

Many stores now offer a wedding list service whereby couples can compile their wedding list from the goods the shop sells and register it with the store. People who wish to give a gift can then visit or telephone the store to select and purchase a present, which is then duly deleted from the wedding list. This should ensure that nothing on the list is duplicated. If a national store is chosen it also means that people living all over the country are able to participate easily because while the couple's local branch will hold the list, branches around the country can ring and check what has yet to be bought, or may be able to call up the list on their computer system, and the guests can make their purchase in their own local store. The greatest benefit of this system is that the store takes on the responsibility of managing the wedding present list, a duty which might otherwise have to be undertaken by the bride's mother, sister or chief bridesmaid.

Cheques are often useful to a newly-married couple who will have a hundred and one needs before they complete their home – but, except in the case of fathers, it is not the kind of present that can be suggested with propriety by the bride or her bridegroom. Tokens from local D-I-Y shops can also be useful for couples who will be decorating their new home.

It is important that track is kept of who sent what. An easy way of keeping such a record is for a note to be made on the gift tag accompanying each of the presents as they are unwrapped (but watch that someone doesn't throw them away with the rubbish!). This will be a great help to the couple when they come to write their thank-you letters.

Arrangements could be made for the display of the wedding presents at the reception, and certainly a table should be set aside to store presents brought to the reception by guests. However, the bride and groom will probably not have time to open any gifts on the day of the wedding itself and they may like to show all their presents in their new home or at the bride's mother's home after the wedding or on their return from honeymoon.

Such an exhibition can be made most attractive; tiers of boxes covered by a white table cloth can do much to set off the beauty and interest of the collection of items. Each present should have a card standing beside it on the display tables, giving the donor's name and brief address (such as: John and Sheila Cox, Sheffield).

In the case of cheques, only an envelope is displayed stating the name and address of the donor but giving no information concerning its value. Under no circumstances should the cheque itself be displayed. It should be paid into the bank!

A similar restriction should be placed on less usual presents such as an insurance policy, the deeds of a house or share certificates which should be filed safely. Simple cards should represent such items on the display tables, endorsed with the words 'Insurance Policy', 'Deeds of House', or 'Shares Certificate' and the name and brief address of the donor.

Whether a display is made at the reception or not, the bride's parents should remove all the presents to their own home at the end of the celebration. A suitable display could then be arranged for the benefit of friends and neighbours who did not attend the reception. This may well last until a few days before the end of the newly-married couple's honeymoon at which point the gifts should be taken to the couple's home where they, too, may choose to display them once again for the benefit of their own friends.

Security and insurance of the wedding presents must be considered. If gifts are taken to the reception venue for display they should be kept in a locked room until the reception commences, to prevent theft or damage. It may be worth considering extra insurance to cover the gifts while they are at the reception, being transported and even in the home of the bride's parents if they include some very valuable items.

After the honeymoon it is the bride's duty to write and thank the individual donors of presents. Such letters should be sent out as soon as possible after the return from honeymoon but, where the numbers make the task a lengthy one, a verbal message – even over the telephone – will serve as an interim measure. Yet however close the giver and however fulsome the verbal thanks, a letter in due course is a must.

15

A CHURCH CEREMONY

We will consider the church ceremony by looking first at the Church of England. However, even if the marriage is to take place in a church which is not Church of England, much of what appears in this chapter will apply, so please read on.

A clergyman of the Church of England may not refuse to perform a marriage service so long as he is sure that there is no legal or ecclesiastical objection to it – and, indeed, he must satisfy himself that the law does in fact specifically permit each particular marriage, since to make a knowingly false declaration is a criminal offence.

Any day of the week may be chosen by the couple as their wedding day, including Sundays and even Good Friday, although the Church does discourage weddings during Lent. It is, of course, necessary for the couple to consult the clergyman concerned to make sure that it is convenient to him and that the church is available.

The most popular days for weddings are Fridays and Saturdays, probably both because it gives the couple an extra weekend for their honeymoon and because it is generally more convenient for their guests. Saturday mornings usually result in a queue of wedding parties at most churches (especially in the summer months) and those who wish to marry at a certain time on a specific day should talk to the clergyman of the church about it well in advance of the projected date – generally months ahead. Preferred times are between 11 am and 4 pm to ensure plenty of time for the reception afterwards.

When the couple have decided on a church they should make an appointment to see the clergyman. Very often he will suggest that they attend a marriage preparation course and, among other things, will discuss what form the service will take.

With the Alternative Service Book 1980, those who wish to be unconventional are given much greater scope by this new service, but it can also be conducted in a very traditional manner. The bridal procession and the ceremony of giving away are optional, and full provision is made for the marriage to take place during a service of Holy Communion.

Two sets of vows are included (with or without the promise to 'obey') which the couple may choose to read instead of repeating after the clergyman. During the vows the bride and groom face each other, and words are provided for the bride either after receiving the ring or on giving a ring to the bridegroom.

The service may incorporate prayers which the couple have written or selected in co-operation with the clergyman and they may choose an appropriate reading or readings from the Bible.

During the scripture reading and sermon the bride and bride-groom may sit in chairs that have been specially placed for them.

The service can be tailored to suit each individual couple so that much of the detail will be decided in consultation with the officiating clergyman.

Many clergymen like to go through the service with each couple in church before the wedding day and have a rehearsal so that everyone is clear who stands where, when to move and generally what to expect. The bridal gown is not needed for this purpose, though it is wise to provide some mock bouquets for young bridesmaids so that they may become accustomed to carrying them when rehearsing their part. Similarly, if a train is to be worn by the bride, a few yards of almost any material will suffice for the rehearsal.

Floral Decorations
The clergyman should also be consulted about the decoration of his church. He has the right to the final say in these arrangements, although he is usually happy for the bride to take full control. White flowers and greenery are usual for weddings but coloured flower arrangements are also very popular, often to match or enhance the bridesmaids' dresses. Lilies, roses, carnations,

chrysanthemums and dahlias are often used – with perhaps ferns or evergreens. A vast display is quite unnecessary and any good florist will do the whole thing for you, or perhaps members of the church flower committee may be available to do the arrangements.

Order of Service

A decision has to be made in advance too, concerning the hymns and other music for the service and it is well to consult the organist as soon as possible. Though it is accepted that it is the bride's prerogative to choose the entrance march, hymns, music to be played during the signing of the register and, of course, a wedding march it is obvious that the advice of the clergyman and organist should be taken fully into account. This is particularly applicable where a choir is wanted. (Again, the clergyman has the right to refuse anything which he feels is inappropriate.)

Once all the music has been selected it is possible to arrange the full details of the service on a printed sheet known as the 'Order of Service'. If the bridal couple and the bride's mother complete all these arrangements in good time it is usual to have the Order of Service printed for the use of all who will attend the ceremony. Some couples also like to include details of any readings to be used in the service (book, chapter and verse if from the Bible or title and author if from elsewhere).

Wedding Day Arrangements

On the morning of the wedding the excitement rises. At an early hour the bride will start getting ready, perhaps with her mother's help. An hour or more before the wedding is due to start, the chief bridesmaid should arrive at the bride's home – dressed and ready. She will then help the bride to put the finishing touches to her appearance whilst the bride's mother snatches an opportunity to don her own wedding outfit.

Meanwhile the bridesmaids will begin to congregate at the bride's home; the best man will be arriving at the bridegroom's home, dressed for the ceremony; the ushers will be making ready in their own homes.

Arriving at the church

At least half an hour before the ceremony is due to start, the head usher or groomsman must arrive at the church. Immediately afterwards the other ushers are due and should then receive their final instructions from him.

The head usher will delegate several ushers to direct cars and help them park if necessary. Others will be asked to meet guests at the church door, hand out Order of Service sheets, and conduct the guests to their pews. He will remind them that the bride's mother, brothers and sisters and her grandparents (as appropriate) should be seated in the front pew to the left of the nave facing the altar.

Others of the bride's relatives and friends should be seated on the same side of the church in descending order of relationship and closeness of friendship – so far as is conveniently possible – from the pews immediately behind the bride's mother to the back of the church.

Similarly, the bridegroom's relatives and friends will occupy the pews on the right of the nave. Part of the front row on that side may be needed for the groom and best man before the service and for the best man when the bride and groom go to the altar, so the closer members of his family may have to go in the pews immediately behind.

As a last instruction, the head usher will hand over Order of Service sheets to the other ushers, either to lay in the pews in advance, or, more usually, to hand out as they conduct the wedding party and the guests to their seats.

Meanwhile, the best man should be making quite certain that the bridegroom is properly dressed for his wedding. He should also check the items he must take with him – the wedding ring (or rings) in his waistcoat pocket, money in his hip pocket to pay the marriage fees if they have not been paid at the time of a rehearsal, and the couple's rail, boat or air tickets, passports and hotel reservations in his inside pocket.

He should conduct the bridegroom to the church in order to arrive at least 20 minutes before the service is due to start. They then usually find themselves some secluded spot in which to wait. The clergyman often takes this opportunity to check details for the register.

From about now on, the guests begin to arrive and must be conducted to their seats. (Though in the past it was usual for women always to wear some form of head-dress in church, there is now no obligation on them to do so. However, many women – in particular, the mothers of the bride and groom – will wish to wear a hat as part of their wedding outfit.) Those who have not met for some time, and those who are meeting for the first time, will be inclined to chat at the church door, causing a little obstruction and possibly creating a hold-up when the bride arrives. A gentle hint here and there should get them to their places in ample time, however.

The chief bridesmaid should arrive in company with the other bridesmaids and pages, not less than five minutes before the bride is due. They should gather in the church porch ready to form a procession and, again, though the guests will tend to stop and talk to them, they should be dissuaded as much as possible as time will be getting short.

At the time the bridesmaids arrive, the best man should lead the bridegroom along the nave to the chancel steps – the best man on the bridegroom's right – though often the groom and best man wait in the front pew until the first notes of the wedding march.

The arrival, entrance and procession of the bridal party is one of the high spots of pageantry for the occasion and it is important, therefore, that everybody should be in their places in good time. The bride and her father arrive at the church last but they should be exactly on time. In areas where traffic is busy it is well for them to leave home early, even if it means that they have to cruise around for a few minutes to adjust their arrival to the exactly scheduled time. Great panic can be caused by the bride who arrives early!

Nor must this be an occasion when the bride exercises a woman's right to be late. It would be discourteous to the clergyman, the organist and the guests – not to mention the nervous groom – and besides, it may cause serious delay to someone else's wedding which may be due to take place imme-diately afterwards.

A few photographs may be taken as the bride walks towards the church on her father's arm. The chief bridesmaid should make any last minute adjustments to the bride's dress.

The organist will be alerted to the bride's arrival and move over from the introductory music to the wedding march. With his daughter on his right arm, her father will lead her forward into the body of the church, in slow time – the pages and the bridesmaids taking up their places in the procession, in pairs, with the chief bridesmaid just behind the bride and her father.

The officiating clergyman (and sometimes the choir) may meet the bride at the door and precede her down the aisle or he may await the bride on the chancel steps. During the processional the bride's attention must not wander. Her gaze should be directed towards the clergyman or the altar, until she stands beside her bridegroom. To effect a properly paced procession, the bride and her father should move off with the left foot in time with the march, those following picking up the step as they fall in behind.

The bridegroom and his best man should turn to welcome the bride as she approaches and her father should lead her to the bridegroom's left. As they face the altar and the clergyman, they stand, from left to right: the bride's father, the bride, the bridegroom and the best man.

Once they are in position, with the bridesmaids standing in pairs behind the bride, the chief bridesmaid should step forward (just as her father releases the bride's arm) to take the bouquet and set the bride's veil clear of her face, back over her head. The chief bridesmaid then returns to her place immediately behind the bride, satisfying herself that the bridesmaids and pages are in their places too.

The service and ceremony
At the beginning of the service, once the bridal party is in place in front of the clergyman, a hymn is often sung. This gives the couple an opportunity to relax a little. The clergyman then begins the chosen service, stating the reason for the gathering in the church, the reason for matrimony, followed by a demand to know if there is any impediment to the marriage, first from the congregation, and then from the couple. To guard against malicious allegations the clergyman may demand a bond from anyone alleging impediment.

1. The procession.

2. Positions during the service.

If he is satisfied that there is no legal objection to the union, he will then ask the man:

'Wilt thou have this woman to thy wedded wife, to live together according to God's law in the holy estate of matrimony? Wilt thou love her, comfort her, honour and keep her, in sickness and in health? And, forsaking all other, keep thee only unto her, so long as ye both shall live?'

The man shall answer: 'I will.'

The clergyman then asks the woman:

'Wilt thou have this man to thy wedded husband, to live together according to God's law in the holy estate of matrimony? Wilt thou love him, comfort him, honour and keep him, in sickness and in health? And, forsaking all other, keep thee only to him, so long as ye both shall live?'

The woman shall answer: 'I will.'

The clergyman will then ask:

'Who giveth this woman to be married to this man?'

Immediately, the bride's father passes his daughter's right hand to the clergyman, palm downwards. He passes it into the hand of the bridegroom. The bride's father's part in the service is now ended and he may, if he wishes, drop back and take his place in the front pew beside his wife, as unobtrusively as possible.

The bridegroom will then say after the clergyman:

'I . . . take thee . . . to my wedded wife, to have and to hold from this day forward, for better, for worse: for richer for poorer; in sickness and in health; to love and to cherish, till death us do part, according to God's holy law; and thereto I give thee my troth.'

The pair will free their hands and then the bride will take the right hand of the man in her own right hand and say after the clergyman:

'I . . . take thee . . . to my wedded husband, to have and to hold from this day forward, for better, for worse: for richer, for poorer; in sickness and in health; to love and to cherish, till death us do part, according to God's holy law; and thereto I give thee my troth.'

As they free their hands, the best man takes the wedding ring from his waistcoat pocket and places it on the surface of the open prayer book proffered by the clergyman. After a prayer for the blessing of the ring, the clergyman will offer it to the bridegroom who will take it and place it on the third finger of his bride's left hand. (She should have transferred her engagement ring to her right hand before leaving for the church.)

While the bridegroom holds the ring in place, he must repeat after the clergyman:

'With this ring I thee wed; with my body I thee honour; and all my worldly goods with thee I share: In the Name of the Father, and of the Son, and of the Holy Ghost. Amen.'

It is often the case these days that the bride wishes to give a ring to the bridegroom. When this is so, the best man gives both rings to the clergyman and they are both blessed. The bride puts the ring on the bridegroom's finger after she herself has received the ring he is giving her, either silently or both say the words together.

The above wording is according to the Alternative Services, First Series. Sometimes a couple chooses to be married with the words of the 1662 Prayer Book, which includes the promise by the bride to obey her husband.

(Couples also have the choice of using the wedding service from the Alternative Service Book 1980 in which the introduction and various elements of the service are different. The clergyman may give a short address. A hymn may be sung instead of the psalm. The Alternative Service Book provides for prayers written or chosen by the couple in consultation with the clergyman.)

This concludes the official ceremony and is followed by the nuptial blessing, prayers and a psalm.

As soon as it is over the clergyman or verger will lead the way to the vestry, or sometimes a chapel, followed in procession by the newly-married couple, the bridegroom's father with the bride's mother, the bride's father with the bridegroom's mother, the best man and the chief bridesmaid, the other bridesmaids and pages and perhaps one or two others.

In the vestry the bride signs the register – in her maiden name probably for the last time (though legally she may choose whether or not to take her husband's surname in the future) – followed by her husband, the clergyman and two witnesses, often the best man and the chief bridesmaid. The choice of witnesses should be made well in advance and is limited by the fact that a witness must be over 18 years of age. Everyone should be made aware of who the witnesses are, to prevent any confusion arising when the bridal party go to sign the register.

As soon as the registration is completed, the organist will get the signal and immediately the bridal couple will start the recessional. The bride will walk with her hand on her husband's left arm and with her veil thrown clear of her face. The chief bridesmaid and best man will follow behind the newly-weds, with the rest of the bridesmaids behind them. They are followed by the bride's father with the groom's mother and the bride's mother with the groom's father.

During the recessional there is no reason why the bridal couple should not smile and nod to their friends as they walk slowly down the nave but there must be no pause or conversation inside the church. (The best man may slip out to reach the church door in advance of the bridal party, if the church has a suitable exit, but if this is to happen the chief bridesmaid should be warned in advance so that she isn't confused by his absence.)

It is usually possible to have the church bells pealed for up to half an hour after the ceremony where a church possesses them (and for twenty minutes immediately prior to the ceremony, if so

3. The recessional.

desired). There will, of course, be an extra charge for this and the organist should be consulted, together with the verger.

After the service
There is likely to be considerable delay at this point. As well as the official photographer, a number of friends of the bride and groom will want to take the opportunity to photograph the newly-weds, their bridesmaids, the official party – and, indeed, the church and the rest of the congregation, as it strolls out into the light of day.

As a sort of Master of Ceremonies, the best man needs to keep a check on the time. The whole party is due to arrive at the reception rooms at a pre-stated time and if there is any unnecessary delay, the result might be a cold meal or a very short reception.

Just before the bridal couple get into their car for the journey to the reception, confetti or rice is normally thrown over them. However, if the clergyman requested at the beginning of the service that confetti should not be used because it causes litter, the guests should, of course, refrain from using it.

The best man must make sure that the bride and her husband leave for the reception first, followed in succession by their parents, bridesmaids, family and guests.

He may have one last duty to perform at the church before he himself follows: he may still have to settle the bridegroom's expenses in the form of marriage fees, organist's fees and any other out-of-pocket expenses that may have arisen on the spot. All fees are usually settled well before the day, but, if not, the best man has this duty at the service. If there is no opportunity for him to have a word with the clergyman before or afterwards, there is no objection to the fees being placed in a sealed envelope and given to the verger to be delivered in due course. Fees are generally paid in one lump.

(If, for some particular reason, a clergyman other than the incumbent of the church where the wedding ceremony is to be held is invited to conduct the service, it is usual to pay the marriage fee to each of them. Such an invitation may be extended to a clergyman who happens to be a close relative or a particular friend of either the bride or the bridegroom.)

The best man will need to be at the reception fairly quickly and, if he is wise, he will either have one of the ushers standing by with a car, or arrange for a taxi to be available.

Marriage of Widows and Widowers

Though the ceremony is exactly the same where the bride happens to be a *widow*, tradition calls for less formality and suggests the omission of the full bridal gown, and the veil. Similarly, the bridegroom should wear a dark lounge suit rather than the formal attire often worn at a bride's 'first' wedding. Not later than the day before her 'second' wedding, the bride should remove her 'first' wedding ring – and never wear it again.

The bride is often not supported by bridesmaids though a matron of honour usually attends her, chosen from amongst sisters (her own or the bridegroom's) or close friends. The bridegroom should be attended by a best man. Ushers may be brought in, but as the ceremony is usually less ostentatious and less formal, there is rarely any need for them at a bride's 'second' marriage.

If there is no procession before the service, the matron of honour should wait for the bride at the chancel steps and her only duty is to relieve the bride of her bouquet. Nor is there any obligation on anyone to 'give the bride away', though she may invite her father or some other male relative to do so.

The ceremony tends to be simple but the same restriction need not be placed on the reception afterwards – if there has been some lapse of time since the bride's first husband died. In such a case a wedding cake, floral decorations and speeches are quite permissible. If the wedding takes place within a year of the first husband's death, however, some people might find it more appropriate for the service and the reception afterwards to be confined to members of the bride and bridegroom's family and only a very few friends.

The marriage of a *widower* is much less restricted by convention than in the case of a widow. However, it is still commonly less formal than a first wedding – but the decision is that of the bride. Her wishes should be followed in the matter of the service, the formality, the number of guests and the scale of the reception afterwards.

The bride would be quite in order if she wore a formal bridal gown and a veil, was attended by bridesmaids and was 'given away' by her father.

Divorcees
Though the civil law permits the re-marriage of divorced persons, it is forbidden by the law of the Church of England. Nor can a clergyman be compelled to permit the re-marriage of a divorced person by anyone else in his church.

This means that no marriage service can be performed in a church of the Church of England where either the bride or the bridegroom have a previous partner still living, unless the clergyman is prepared to ignore the church authorities and follow the civil law.

However, ecclesiastical authority does allow for a service of prayer and dedication (often called a 'Blessing Service') which may follow a civil wedding. This must not pretend to be a wedding and there are no legal formalities. This service of blessing can be held in a church, or before the reception at the bride's home, in a marquee, hotel or hired hall, if the clergyman is willing to officiate.

Double Wedding
That is, the marriage of two couples before the same clergyman (or Superintendent Registrar of Marriages) at the same time and in the same ceremony. This is by no means a rare occurrence.

Less common are ceremonies binding three separate couples in wedlock at the same time.

Larger groups are not unknown and, indeed, there is nothing to prohibit a mass wedding, linking together any number of couples at the same time. However, the cause for such massive ceremonies is rare in this country and multiple weddings are more often than not confined to family celebrations. Most common of all such occasions is the simultaneous marriage of sisters, or of twins, to their chosen partners.

A double wedding calls for precisely the same detailed prior arrangements as those applicable to anybody about to marry. Each one of them must give the same notice; each couple must be separately licenced and, of course, distinct certificates of marriage will be issued to each of the couples.

The brides will have their own bridesmaids and a best man will be chosen by each of the bridegrooms. The brides will walk down the aisle side-by-side to join their waiting bridegrooms. The two couples will then stand before the clergyman side-by-side, each bridegroom on the right of his bride.

The single ceremony will embrace both couples and only the responses will be made individually.

The recession must generally be made in separate parties because of the narrowness of the usual aisle, each party being complete in itself. The leading couple will assume that place by arrangement and not because of any 'right', though it is usual to allow the elder of the two men to escort his bride and their attendants from the church first.

Video Recordings of the Ceremony
Many couples like to have a video tape taken of their wedding day, including the ceremony and often the reception afterwards. This could be done by the official photographer or some other person but the clergyman and the organist should be consulted about this in advance of the wedding day in case there are any restrictions. The clergyman has the legal right to have the final say, although most are happy for this to take place provided the video camera operator will be discreet and unobtrusive. There may also be copyright implications regarding the hymns and any other music played during the service (the organist will be able to give advice on such matters). Also, the Parochial Church Council will normally charge a fee for the use of a video camera in church (the clergyman will be able to give exact details).

16

THE CEREMONY BY OTHER RITES, AND CIVIL MARRIAGES

The Roman Catholic Church

There are two types of service for those marrying within the rites of the Roman Catholic church: the 'Marriage celebrated during Mass' and the 'Marriage celebrated outside Mass'.

In each ceremony the first part is identical. This consists of the Entrance Rite, the Liturgy of the Word, and the Rite of Marriage. Where the Mass is to be celebrated, the Liturgy of the Eucharist follows during which it is customary for the Catholics who are present to receive Holy Communion.

In the Roman Catholic Church a 'mixed marriage' is one between a Roman Catholic and someone who has been baptised in another Christian church, and a marriage between a Roman Catholic and someone who has not been baptised.

A marriage celebrated during Mass is usually considered appropriate in a marriage between Roman Catholics. A couple in a mixed marriage may discuss this with the priest.

A marriage between a Catholic and a baptised non-Catholic requires express permission from the Catholic party's parish priest. A marriage between a Catholic and a non-baptised person needs a dispensation, obtainable through the parish priest.

In either case the Catholic party has to undertake to avoid the danger of falling away from the faith, and sincerely to promise to do everything possible 'within the unity of the partnership' to ensure the Catholic baptism and upbringing of all children of the marriage. Also, the priest must be able to sign a statement saying that, in his opinion, the non-Catholic will not oppose the fulfilment of the promise made by the Catholic. Such a marriage will normally take place in the Catholic church; for good reasons, a dispensation *can* be granted for it to be celebrated in the church of the other Christian partner.

In any event it is essential for the couple to consult the clergyman who is to conduct the service at least six months in advance. This gives plenty of time for the ironing out of any 'snags' that may exist, ensures that the date and time of the ceremony can be fixed without clashing with any other arrangements and allows the clergyman to prepare both parties before marrying them in his church. Indeed, it is increasingly common for all couples who are marrying in the Catholic Church to be asked to attend some form of 'preparation'. This is wider than 'religious instruction', and covers a number of points which are common to *all* marriages. The purpose of this is to try to ensure that the couple are prepared adequately for marriage and have a reasonable understanding of what they are doing.

It is customary in both forms of the Catholic marriage service for the bride to be accompanied into the church either by one of her parents or a near relative. The bride is accompanied to the bridegroom standing before the altar, with the best man on his right. It is also possible for the bride and bridegroom to enter the church together, and be greeted at the entrance by the priest and members of the family. The couple may then lead family and friends into the church. The current Rite of Marriage allows for both forms of entry. The Rite also allows for both the traditional gesture in which the bride is 'given away' by her father (or whoever accompanied her into the church) or, alternatively, for the bride simply to offer her hand to the bridegroom. The chief bridesmaid stations herself slightly behind the bride, on her left, after attending to the wedding veil and taking charge of the bridal bouquet. The bridesmaids stand in a line behind, facing the altar.

After the exchange of vows there follows the blessing of the ring(s). The husband places the ring on his wife's finger with the words: '. . . (Christian name only), take this ring as a sign of my love and fidelity. In the name of the Father, and of the Son, and of the Holy Spirit.' If there are two rings, the wife places a ring on her husband's finger saying the same words. At the end of the ceremony the bridal couple sign the register accompanied by at least two witnesses.

The bride and bridegrooms will need to choose music, hymns and readings to be used in the service, in consultation with the priest (and the organist). They will be invited to read out the passages from the scripture themselves during the ceremony or to invite relatives or friends to do so. The priest or deacon will read the Gospel passage. This is where the couple can bring their own personal 'touch' to the proceedings, by choosing a piece from the scripture, hymns and music which have, perhaps, special meaning for them. Naturally, if the scripture passage and music chosen are pertinent to the wedding service, so much the better, and this can make the whole proceedings fuller and richer. The selected readings can be included on the Order of Service sheets if they have been selected far enough in advance (book, chapter and verse if from the Bible or title and author if from elsewhere).

On signing the register the bride will use her maiden name, probably for the last time (although, legally, she does not have to take the name of her husband upon marriage). The witnesses who are to sign the register should be chosen well in advance; this prevents any confusion arising when the chosen group proceed to the Sanctuary. The usual persons chosen to accompany the bridal pair as witnesses of the signatures are the best man and the chief bridesmaid, but in any event, each person who is to act as a witness should be 18 years of age or over. Bear this in mind if you have chosen a particularly young chief bridesmaid or best man.

When the ceremony is concluded, the protocol afterward, when the bride and bridegroom leave the Sanctuary, is for the brides-maids and best man to take up places behind the bridal couple – the chief bridesmaid on the right arm of the best man, other bridesmaids and pageboys following in pairs. The procession then moves in the recessional down the aisle to the church door. Now is the time for the photographers to move in and snap the group, including the wedding guests who have now left the church door.

Afterwards, the whole party proceeds to the scene of the wedding reception.

The re-marriage of divorced persons is strictly refused in the

Catholic Church. However, there may be cases where a previous marriage is not recognised by the Church: when a declaration of nullity of the previous marriage has been granted by the Catholic Church, or if a previous marriage has not complied with Church Law. In these cases, a church marriage would normally be permitted.

The Free Churches
In the majority of Free Church denominations the church itself will have been registered by a Superintendent Registrar of Marriages as a building in which marriages may be solemnised. Ministers of the United Reformed Church, the Baptist, Methodist and other Protestant churches have long taken advantage of their rights, under the Marriage Act of 1898, to become registered as 'authorised' persons; that is, to have applied for and received sanction both to conduct the service and to act as the registrar under the civil law.

Others, for various reasons, have not sought such authority and, in consequence, though they may conduct a marriage ceremony, a superintendent registrar or his deputy must be present to record the wedding, or a separate civil ceremony must be conducted by a superintendent registrar in his office.

Whether or not the minister conducting the service is an authorised person, proper notice of the intention to marry must be given in accordance with civil law and the service must take place in a registered building. Also, wherever the venue of a marriage, the register must be signed by the bridal couple after they have made their vows and the fact must be acknowledged by the signatures of two witnesses.

The minister concerned should be consulted well in advance of the projected date of the wedding so that the church can be booked and in order to ensure plenty of time for all the other necessary arrangements to be made. In all cases, the order of service is a matter left almost entirely to the religious scruples of the couple who are to be married, and, of course, to the special rites of the church whose blessing they seek. At some point in the service, however, declarations must be made in the presence of the minister (or some authorised member of the church) or before

a registrar in the couple's choice of the following prescribed
words:

i) Declaratory words
   'I do solemnly declare that I know not of any lawful
   impediment why I . . . may not be joined in matrimony
   to . . .'

or

   'I declare that I know of no legal reason why I . . . may not
   be joined in marriage to . . .'

or

   by replying 'I am' to the question: 'Are you . . . free lawfully
   to marry . . .?'

ii) Contracting words (to each other in turn)
   'I call upon these persons here present to witness that I . . . do
   take thee . . . to my lawful wedded husband (or wife).'

or

   'I . . . take you . . . to be my wedded wife (or husband).'

or

   'I . . . take thee . . . to be my wedded wife (or husband).'

The differences between the ceremonies of the different denominations are considerable – sometimes merely a matter of detail,
sometimes they are fundamental. Some churches are more ornate
in their ceremonial than others, some more formal and yet others
are extremely simple. In almost every case, however, the order of
service roughly follows that customary in the Church of England,
some details of which include:

1. The procession during which the bride enters and comes to
    stand before the minister, to the left of her bridegroom, her
    father (or whoever is to give her away) on her left. The best
    man stands on the right of the bridegroom.
2. The service usually begins with a prayer and a hymn,
    followed by a declaration of the purpose of marriage.
3. The minister will call upon the congregation to voice any
    legal objection to the marriage.

4. The couple exchange vows as required by law and then give
    and receive a ring or rings.
5. The couple receive the blessing of the church.
6. The register is signed by the couple and two witnesses.
7. The bridal party leave the church to the recessional.

The minister (and organist) should be consulted before any Order
of Service sheet is printed, regarding the selection of hymns,
music and readings and the order in which things will take place
throughout the service.

Although it is general for the Free Churches to view a marriage
as binding for life, it is usually within the discretion of each
minister to consider the re-marriage of a divorced person, exam-
ining each individual case in the light of its own merits.

Some ministers may be adamant in their refusal to marry a
person who has been divorced, others will take note of who was
the injured party and yet others may consider the whole circumstances surrounding the breakdown of a former marriage. Where
one of the couple is divorced, therefore, careful enquiries need to
be made before any arrangements are completed.

It should be remembered that although the clergyman of a
Parish Church *must* conduct the marriage of any couple legally
free to marry (both parties marrying for the first time), a Free
Church minister does not have to. He may impose a faith
requirement and may refuse to conduct the marriage service for
reason of lack of faith on the part of the engaged couple.

The Quakers (Religious Society of Friends)
A Quaker marriage is very different from most other wedding
services. It is extremely simple and altogether free of ceremonial.

The first step to such a marriage needs to be taken at least six
weeks in advance of the proposed date when application should
be made to the registering officer of the monthly meeting within
the bounds of which it is proposed that the marriage should take
place. For each non-Quaker applicant, support in writing must be
obtained from two adult members of the Society, given on forms
which the registering officer will supply; if the registering officer
assents to the application he will supply the party or parties with

the appropriate form for the superintendent registrar.

The couple must then make application to marry in accordance with civil law through the Superintendent Registrar of Marriages in the district in which they live – or if they live in different districts, notice must be given to the registrar in each district.

Notice of the intended marriage is given by the Quaker registering officer at the Sunday morning meeting or meetings to which the parties belong or which they usually attend or in the area in which they live. If no written objection is received, the registering officer will ask the appropriate meeting to appoint a meeting for worship for the solemnisation of the marriage. Public notice of such a meeting will be given at the place at which it is to be held, at the close of the previous meeting for worship.

The service, as any Quaker meeting, is held on the basis of silent communication of the spirit: there is neither pageantry nor music, set service nor sermon; there is, however, opportunity for those who may feel moved by the spirit to give a spoken message of prayer. There is not necessarily a bridesmaid or a best man; a morning coat is unusual and the bride's dress will be fairly simple; there is neither a procession nor a recessional afterwards. But at some point during the meeting the bride and groom will rise and, hand-in-hand, make their declaration of marriage.

The bridegroom will say:

'Friends, I take this my friend . . . to be my wife, promising, through divine assistance, to be unto her a loving and faithful husband, so long as we both on earth shall live.'

The bride makes a similar declaration. The wedding certificate is then signed by the bridal couple and by two of the witnesses. The certificate is read aloud by the registering officer and after the meeting it is usual for all others present to add their names to it. The wedding ring plays no official part in the marriage, though it is common for the couple either to exchange rings afterwards or for the groom to give one to his bride.

It is usual at the close of the meeting for worship for the couple to withdraw with four witnesses and the registering officer to complete the civil marriage register.

The Society retains its belief in the sanctity and life-long nature of marriage, but recognises that in certain circumstances it may be right to make a new start, and the re-marriage of a divorced person may be allowed at the discretion of the monthly meeting.

The Jewish wedding

Synagogue marriage in Britain is both a civil and religious ceremony. The requirements of both must be satisfied before the marriage can take place. Two separate applications for permission to marry are necessary.

Each party makes a personal visit, about twelve weeks before the wedding, to the register office of their home district. After 21 days the superintendent registrar issues his Certificate of Marriage. This must be sent or brought to the office authorising the synagogue marriage. Marriage at short notice can be arranged by a special licence obtainable from the registrar for an additional fee.

Those wishing to marry under the auspices of the Chief Rabbi must attend the Marriage Authorisation Office (see Appendix for address) or the religious authority under which their ceremony is to take place. This meeting should occur 3–4 months prior to the proposed wedding date. Outside London, the local Minister or Secretary for Marriages can arrange this.

Normally on the Sabbath prior to the wedding, the bridegroom is called up to the Reading of the Law in Synagogue.

It is customary for bride and groom to fast on the wedding day until after the ceremony, although there are some days in the Jewish calendar which are exceptions to this rule.

Etiquette at the Synagogue can vary. However, the groom is always expected to arrive first. He sits in a place of honour, sometimes the seats allocated to the Wardens of the Synagogue, with his father, future father-in-law and best man.

The groom takes his place first under the *chuppah* (wedding canopy), the best man stands behind and to his left, ready to hand over the ring.

The bride can be brought in either by her father and mother, or by her mother and the groom's mother, followed by bridesmaids and other relatives. There is no hard and fast rule. The *Unterfuhrers*, as those who accompany the bride and groom are called, also stand beneath the *chuppah*.

Before the bride comes under the *chuppah* the groom is formally requested by the Minister to approve the appointment of two witnesses who sign the *ketubah* (marriage document) and accept the terms and conditions of the *ketubah* whereby he undertakes a number of obligations to his wife. The bride stands under the *chuppah* at the groom's right.

The ceremony begins with a chant of welcome, followed by the blessings of betrothal which are recited over a cup of wine. The first blessing is for the wine itself and the second praises God for the commandment to marry and the implicit restrictions which concern any forbidden marriages. If the Minister wishes to give spiritual guidance and personal blessing to the couple, he will do this before the commencement of the blessings of betrothal.

In Jewish law, the couple become married when the man places the ring on the woman's finger and makes the declaration 'Behold thou art consecrated unto me by this ring according to the Law of Moses and of Israel.' The woman's consent is signified by her acceptance of the ring. It is important to note that this act effecting their union is carried out by the parties themselves; it is not the Minister who 'marries' them, but they who marry each other, and the Minister's presence is as a Jewish law expert, and sometimes as witness to the *ketubah* as well as in a civil capacity if he is Secretary for Marriages.

Since the ring has such importance, it must be the groom's property, should be circular in make and in precious metal (but without jewels), and the bride should wear no other rings or jewellery during the ceremony. The ring is placed on the bride's right index finger, but she may transfer it to the 'ring finger' later. The reason for Jewish insistence on a plain ring is to allow no difference between rich and poor and to avoid any deception or misunderstanding as to its value. It is placed on the right index finger because in ancient transactions this finger was used symbolically to acquire things.

The *ketubah* is now read out loud in Aramaic original. An English abstract follows. The bride should look after the *ketubah* carefully since it is her interests which it recognises, and should it be lost she should get it replaced.

Then follow the Seven Blessings of Marriage, recited over a cup of wine. These words of prayer call upon the Almighty to help the bride and groom find the perfect happiness of Adam and Eve and live a life of 'joy and gladness, mirth and exultation, pleasure and delight, love and brotherhood, peace and companionship'. The couple then sip wine from separate cups given to them by their respective mothers-in-law. This is followed by the breaking of a glass by the groom – a custom that dates back to Talmudic times.

The ceremony concludes by the Minister pronouncing the blessing of the Priests found in the Bible, in the heartfelt wish that its words of blessing, protection, grace and peace be fulfilled for bride and groom.

The couple sign the civil marriage documents, the bride signing her maiden name. The group leave the Synagogue in procession with their attendants. Before greeting their guests at the reception they will spend a short period of time together in private (*yihud*) denoting their newly-acquired status as husband and wife, entitled to live together under the same roof. Having (in most cases) been fasting since dawn on the day of their wedding, they will now break their fast and have their first meal together as husband and wife.

Civil marriages

Nowadays, more and more people are choosing to marry through a civil ceremony. There are many reasons for this – perhaps because the couple have no religious beliefs, or perhaps one or both of the parties is divorced, or perhaps for other reasons.

Before the issue of a Superintendent Registrar's Certificate, 21 days must elapse following the giving of notice. Where the couple apply for a Superintendent Registrar's Licence and satisfy the requirements for the issue of such a document the ceremony may be performed by the superintendent registrar after the expiration of one clear working day, except a Sunday, Good

Friday or Christmas Day, from the date of the entry of the notice.
(See Chapter 3 for the legal requirements with regard to the issue
of a Superintendent Registrar's Certificate or Licence.)

Such a marriage entails no religious service; all that is
expected is that the couple's choice of the following vows be
exchanged before a superintendent registrar and two witnesses:

> 'I do solemnly declare that I know not of any lawful
> impediment why I, . . ., may not be joined in matrimony
> to . . .'

or

> 'I declare that I know of no legal reason why I, . . ., may not
> be joined in marriage to . . .'

or

> by replying 'I am' to the question 'Are you . . . free lawfully
> to marry . . .?'

The couple must also say to each other one of the following
statements:

> 'I call upon these persons here present to witness that I, . . .,
> do take thee, . . ., to be my lawful wedded wife (or hus-
> band)'.

or

> 'I . . . take you . . . to be my wedded wife (or husband).'

or

> 'I . . . take thee . . . to be my wedded wife (or husband).'

Then follows the signing of the marriage register by each of the
newly-weds and those witnessing the event.

The symbol of the wedding ring(s), given by the bridegroom to
the bride or exchanged between the couple, is common practice
but has no legal significance under civil law.

A register office wedding can be as informal or as dressy as the
parties concerned wish to make it. It can be a very simple and
small affair, with informal dress, and perhaps just the two
necessary witnesses accompanying the bride and groom. On the
other hand, it may be conducted in full bridal regalia (the bride in

a long white dress, attended by bridesmaids and pages, and the groom, best man and male guests in morning dress); as many guests as can be accommodated in the wedding room can attend the ceremony; there can be flower arrangements to complement the bridal party; everything can be done to make the ceremony as 'special' as possible. (It has been known for brides to arrive at some register offices in horse drawn carriages or white Rolls Royces.)

However, a register office wedding is restricted in many ways – size of room, lack of time, uninspiring surroundings – and many people prefer to take advantage of the 1994 Marriage Act (England and Wales) which allows a civil wedding to take place in any approved premises (see page 28). This means that the wedding ceremony can be personalised and extended to a much greater degree than is possible in a busy register office. Again, no religious element is allowed because it is a civil ceremony but the couple may add secular readings and music and generally make it special in their own way, provided due regard is given to the solemn nature of the event. In many instances the ceremony and reception both take place in the same building, although that is not necessarily the case.

The superintendent registrar should be consulted if a civil wedding is planned – either in a register office or in some other approved premises. (A book listing all the approved premises in England and Wales is available for purchase from the office of the Registrar General in Southport, but a list of venues in each registration district is available from the local register office.) Possible dates should be discussed with the registrar as well as the chosen venue for both the wedding and the reception in advance of any firm bookings being made because a registrar will need to be available to conduct the ceremony (and two will have to attend a civil ceremony which is not held in a register office).

The civil law takes no notice of religious beliefs or scruples in the case of the re-marriage of divorcees. So long as the decree absolute has been granted and all other legal requirements have been met, the superintendent registrar is duty bound to perform such a marriage ceremony.

17

CELEBRATIONS

After the wedding ceremony comes the reception and this can be as formal or informal as the couple wish to make it. The main criteria will be how much money is to be spent and how many guests have to be invited. This will help make the decision as to whether the reception is to be held in the bride's home, quite often with a marquee in the garden to give added space, in a village or church hall where there are usually tables, chairs, cloakrooms and kitchen facilities already, or in a restaurant or hotel which provide all the necessary services including a room where the bride can change into her going away outfit.

The modern house is generally too small in which to entertain more than a limited number of guests, and rarely big enough to accommodate all those who expect and feel entitled to be invited.

This can be overcome by hiring a marquee or lean-to awning to extend the space available and these normally come in widths of 20, 30 and 40 feet in length. Many firms provide coloured roof and wall linings complete with chandeliers, wall bracket lights or spot lights, and both matting and wooden flooring are available. Such firms will also provide chairs and tables and a range of heaters, should the wedding be during the cold months. (It is becoming increasingly common for families who have hired a marquee to hold a reception followed by a disco in the evening.)

If the bride's mother is a good and highly organised cook it is quite possible for her to prepare and freeze food beforehand and she will need to choose items that can be served easily so that she is not trying to be cook, waitress and hostess on the day. She will also have to hire or borrow enough chairs, small tables, china and cutlery, and organise a wine waiter or two, perhaps from the local off-licence who will be supplying the wine and glasses. Alternatively, a firm of caterers can be brought in who will suggest suitable menus, provide the linen, china and silver as well as serving the food and clearing up afterwards. Most caterers will also serve and deal with the drinks even if they have not provided the wine or the glasses. The bride's mother will also have to organise the flowers and table decorations or arrange for the caterers to take on this responsibility.

If the house is large enough, a room should be set aside for the display of the wedding presents as this gives guests the opportunity to inspect the presents and provides a 'quiet' room away from most of the bustle for the two families to get to know one another better.

The hall will be needed as a reception room where the host and hostess can receive and welcome their guests. The bride's brother and sisters, the bridesmaids and the best man should be briefed to keep the flow of guests passing beyond the reception point towards the main room without pause. As they arrive the guests should shake hands with the bride's mother first and then her father. Immediately afterwards they meet the bridegroom's parents followed by the bride and bridegroom, in that order. To prevent any hold-ups everyone should make their greetings brief and save longer conversations until after all the guests have been received. At large weddings this can take a long time so sometimes the reception line is dispensed with, and the guests are received briefly by bride and groom only.

At this point the guests will be offered a drink – sherry, still or sparkling white wine, with apple, grape or orange juice for those who want it – and they will circulate until the bride and bridegroom make a move towards the buffet table, or, if it is to be a sit down meal, to their places at the top table (see Fig. 4). When the bride and groom have been served or served themselves from the table, it is the general signal for everyone else to do so and they can then either circulate with their food, or take it to a table and join other guests in an informal way.

Where a luncheon or other meal is to be served, the bride and bridegroom sit at the head of the table, the bride on her husband's left. The bride's mother sits next to the bridegroom and the

4. The top table.

bridegroom's mother on the left of the bride's father who sits next to his newly-married daughter. The best man and the chief bridesmaid complete the top table as shown in Fig. 4. Alternatively, the best man and chief bridesmaid can take places beside the bride and groom, with the parents further out from the centre, in which case the table would look like Fig. 5. If the groom's parents and bride's parents prefer to sit each beside their own partners, then this can be accommodated with the layout of Fig. 6.

Depending on the spaces available, the caterer will suggest how the tables and chairs can best be placed so that all those who

5. Alternative top table.

wish to sit down can do so. Where there is to be a 'serve yourself' buffet, the cake and the bride's bouquet are put at one end, and the bride and groom will stand to one side of the cake during the speeches and toasts.

If the reception is held in a village hall, town hall or other rooms, an area needs to be kept clear in which the guests are greeted and here again a caterer will be able to suggest the best way of arranging the room or rooms.

Most medium and large hotels have the facilities and often specialise in the organisation of wedding receptions. Their staff will cook and serve almost any meal desired; they will provide

6. Another alternative.

the wines and give advice on the subject; they will arrange the tables, the decorations, cloakrooms, the reception room, the dining room, and, if required, a room for the display of the wedding presents.

Their commissionaire, or doorman, should be outside on the pavement ready to open car doors – and to keep a space free of parked vehicles immediately opposite the entrance.

The hall porter will be ready to direct the guests to the apartments allocated for the function and the cloakroom attendants ready to receive the coats.

Sherry, white wine (or champagne) and non-alcoholic fruit

juices will be poured into glasses ready to be served as the guests arrive and the waitresses briefed to move among them with trays prepared and loaded with the reception drinks.

Arrangements for all receptions need to be made well in advance. The host and hostess will have to decide on the following:

(a) The time and date.
(b) The menu.
(c) The wines and soft drinks to be served.
(d) Who is to make and ice the cake?
(e) What flowers are to be used on the tables and who provides them?
(f) The number of guests to be present.
(g) The seating plan, if one is needed.
(h) Whether they require a room in which the bride can change into her going away outfit.

A reception after the wedding ceremony is intended to allow the guests to congratulate the newly-weds, to join in the toasts to the health and happiness of the couple, to witness the cutting of the cake and to wish them well as they leave for their honeymoon. It is also an opportunity for the two families to get to know each other better.

The meal itself is incidental to the celebrations and is served because the guests will be hungry long before the bride and bridegroom leave for their honeymoon – especially if they have travelled any distance to attend the wedding. As the meal has always been an essential need, it has long been the custom to use it for the high-spot feature of the celebrations. During it, the toasts are given, the cake cut and the greetings messages read to the guests. Because of this, all the arrangements need a great deal of thought and careful planning.

There are many methods and fashions in which to conduct a ceremonial wedding breakfast and/or evening reception. Few of the arrangements are obligatory, though custom lays down certain broad highlights. The main thing to remember is that it is the day of the newly-weds.

Advance Arrangements

The wedding cake
The cake must be ordered many weeks in advance of the wedding and apart from the style and decorations, its size should be considered in relation to the number of guests expected to attend the reception and those who will expect to receive a portion who were unable to be present. It is quite common for the cake to be home-made and professionally iced. It should be delivered to the caterer at the reception rooms in good time – either the night before or early on the wedding day itself.

The flowers
Flower arrangements may be part of the package that the caterer offers. If not, the caterer will be glad to receive the flowers that have been ordered by the bride's mother for the tables as early as possible on the morning of the reception. Besides flowers for the tables, one or two large arrangements may be necessary and a florist will always provide these if the family has no good 'flower arranging' friends. If a posy is required for the top of the wedding cake this can also be provided by the florist.

Menus and other printed material
Details of the menus and wines will have been settled weeks in advance of the wedding date between the hosts and the caterer or hotelier. If menus are required these should be ordered and printed then (although a hotel may provide these as part of a wedding reception package), along with paper serviettes with the names or initials of the bride and bridegroom, place cards, drink mats, ash trays and book matches, as required. Samples of these items can be seen at any large stationers and can be ordered through them to meet individual requirements. Whatever is ordered should be in the hands of the caterer the day before the wedding – not forgetting the need to write the guests' names on the place cards.

The reception rooms
Although the rooms required for the reception will have been agreed with the caterer and booked some time in advance there

are still a few arrangements which must be completed by the host. If a hall has been hired, it is as well to check with the caretaker that the hall will have been cleaned the day before, that there are adequate tables and chairs, whether or not the hall provides towels and soap in the cloakrooms and whether the hall has its own flower vases for larger arrangements.

If the wedding presents are to be displayed the caterer will need to know how many trestle tables will be required and if a separate room is used it should be cleared of unnecessary furniture. On the afternoon before the wedding the bride's parents, the bride and bridegroom and possibly the best man will make a display of the gifts, making sure to keep the wrappings and boxes so that they can be transported safely after the wedding reception.

If the presents are valuable, they should be insured to include their display. A hotelier will do his best to safeguard them overnight and during the reception, but he is unlikely to accept responsibility for theft or damage; caterers coming into a hall booked by the hosts will take no responsibility for them whatsoever. The room should be locked overnight and unlocked as the guests are due to arrive. It is up to the bridal party to remove the presents afterwards (see page 91).

The seating arrangements
The caterer will need to have a general idea of how many guests are to be entertained some time in advance of the event – and he should be given final details, together with the seating plan and the place-cards, not later than the evening before the wedding. There are certain formalities concerning the seating arrangements, though a hostess should not distress herself if she finds it more convenient, or a happier solution, to seat people in some other manner. This plan cannot be made without the assistance of the caterer who will advise on the layout of the tables to suit the numbers involved, the shape and style of the room and the service points.

The top table is the most important and the main preoccupation of the planner, and the simplest arrangements are those already given on page 122. So far as other guests are concerned, brothers and sisters should be interspersed by their wives and husbands (where applicable). Uncles and aunts follow and then the friends of the newly-weds. The length of the side tables will depend largely on the size and shape of the room and the number of guests to be seated.

If there is plenty of room, only the outer sides should be used so that everybody has a clear view of everybody else. Usually this is impracticable – or it would make the tables stretch out to such a length that those towards the foot of each arm will be out of touch with the top table. In such case the inner sides of the arms should be used.

Under no circumstances should the inner side of the top table be used for seating purposes. The cake, on a small separate table in front of the bridal couple, should be the only thing to screen their faces. Even this is often placed to one corner of the room.

Of course, even larger layouts may be used, and for numbers in excess of, perhaps, 200, an attractive arrangement can be made with separate tables set at an angle to the top table, so that not one of the guests will have their backs fully turned towards the newly-weds. (Fewer guests in a small room can also be accommodated in this way.) This plan can be extended to suit the room, either by adding extra sprigs if the room is long, or by lengthening them if it is broad. However, the caterer will have expert knowledge and his advice should be sought.

The variety of possible seating arrangements for the guests is almost infinite, depending on whether the meal is a self-service buffet or a waitress-served sit-down meal. A buffet can be completely informal, with guests eating on the move or sitting anywhere at tables or simply on chairs provided; or a seating plan can be given, with everyone allocated a specific place to sit, as would happen for a sit-down, waitress served meal. However the guests are seated, the one thing that must happen is that the bridal party will have a table, known as the 'top table' at which to sit. This will face the guests and may well display the wedding cake too.

After due consideration has been given to the arrangement for seating the members of the two families, their husbands and wives, and the friends of the bride and bridegroom, an attempt should be made to alternate the sexes as far as possible. A good hostess will also give thought to the problem of family feuds, jealousies and friendships. Such likes and dislikes, if they are not sorted out before the reception, may well lead to quarrels, unhappy silences and outspoken comments. To separate anti-pathetic guests, irrespective of their seating 'rights', is much better than to leave matters to take their course and hope for the best. This is the newly-weds' 'day' and every effort must be made to keep it free of friction. 'Off-beat' guests might well be kept at a distance from the top table, humorists kept apart and younger couples with a personal interest in one another placed happily side-by-side.

The suggestion is that the bride's family and friends should occupy the tables on the bridegroom's side of the room – and vice versa, but others will persuade the host and hostess that the families should be mixed as freely as possible. Both arrangements have a lot to commend them to the hostess. Mixing the families does tend to give them an opportunity to get to know one another, while segregation may mean less embarrassment to all concerned.

The table plan, with places marked with the name of a guest, should be given to the caterer to post up in a convenient place so that the guests will be able to go straight to their places as they enter the dining room – and confirm the actual seat by means of the place-card bearing his or her name lying on the table by the place.

The Arrival
Though the newly-weds leave the church first, it is important that the bride's parents arrive first at the reception. As host and hostess they must be the first to greet their guests as they arrive, if there is to be a reception line.

The reception line should consist of:

The bride's mother
The bride's father
The bridegroom's mother
The bridegroom's father
The bride
The bridegroom

in that order.

If the reception is to include a buffet meal, the official greeting by both sets of parents and the newly-weds almost invariably takes place immediately on the arrival of the guests, but if there is to be a luncheon, it is quite usual for this greeting of the guests to take place later, as they pass into the dining room.

This is often preferred as it relieves the parents and the newly-weds of the duty to rush to the reception rooms from the ceremony and gives the bride time to recover composure. It also enables the photographer to take his pictures of the cutting of the cake while the guests remove their coats and prepare themselves to meet other guests before passing along the reception line.

Assume that the official greeting is to take place immediately on the arrival of the guests: in this case, guests are welcomed by their hosts and the bridal couple as they arrive – without regard to family seniority. The greetings must be brief if there is not to be a long line of impatiently waiting guests and the best man and bridesmaids should do their best to move them on by directing them towards the already poured drinks.

They should be encouraged, too, to circulate about the room, to meet one another – and, of course, take the opportunity to inspect the wedding presents.

The guests should arrive as promptly as possible so that the bridal party can finish with the greetings and then lead the guests towards the meal.

The Wedding Meal
As soon as the last guest has been received, the best man should lead the couple and other members of the bridal party to where their guests are conversing and enjoying a drink. They may join them for a while but must avoid standing in cliques and not allow any one person to monopolise their attention.

They may spend a few minutes inspecting their wedding presents and discussing them with their guests – but the best man must keep his eye on the time.

As soon as the caterer or one of his staff indicates that the meal is ready, he should persuade the newly-weds to move towards the tables arm-in-arm. Behind the newly-weds, the bridal party should be in the following order:

The bride's father with the bridegroom's mother.
The bridegroom's father with the bride's mother.
The best man with the chief bridesmaid.
The bridesmaids.
The pages.

And, finally, the guests.

Before entering the dining room the guests should have examined the seating plan and so, with the help of the place-cards, should have little difficulty in locating their seats.

When everybody has found his or her place, the best man should obtain silence and if 'grace' is to be said, call upon the clergyman or minister present to 'say grace'. Often, in the absence of a clergyman or minister, a known member of a church among the guests may be invited to do this duty but he or she should be approached in advance, not on the day itself. Failing any of these arrangements the task should be undertaken by the bride's father. One of the following forms of words would be suitable:

(a) *For our families, our friends and for this food which you give us, we thank you Lord.*
(b) *Receive our thanks, O Lord, for this food and for this happy day.*
(c) *We thank you, our Father, for good food which brings health, and human love which brings happiness.*
(d) *For what we are about to receive, may the Lord make us truly thankful and ever mindful of the needs of others.*

Grace is often neglected nowadays, and may not be appropriate at a reception following a civil wedding. However, after a church wedding if a minister of religion is present the grace should never be omitted.

The Speeches
As soon as the guests appear to have reached the end of their meal, the toasts are drunk. Unless an official toastmaster is

present the best man takes on this role and calls on the first speaker when he thinks the time is ripe.

The bride's father

The first speech is given either by a close personal friend or by a relative of the bride – usually her father. The toast is: 'The Health and Happiness of the Bride and Bridegroom'.

Though it is usual for this toast to be given by the bride's father – or guardian – it is not uncommon for that duty to be passed to some other male member of the bride's family who is deemed to be perhaps a better speaker or is someone of note. But the bride's father must remember to delegate such a task some days in advance and not spring it on an unsuspecting guest at the last moment.

The speech is usually of a semi-serious nature, especially if it is made by the father and generally includes:

1. The happiness he and his wife have experienced in bringing up their daughter, the treasure she has been to them and the loss they will feel following her marriage and move to a home of her own.
2. A couple of interludes in her life – one perhaps amusing, the other more serious.
3. A welcome into the family to the new son-in-law and an expression of the hope that it will be gaining a son rather than losing a daughter.
4. A welcome, too, to the bridegroom's parents.
5. Perhaps an episode concerning the bride and the bridegroom together – particularly if they have known one another for a number of years.
6. A little timely advice to the newly-weds, usually bound up with his own experiences in company with his wife – the bride's mother.
7. The toast to the Health and Happiness of the couple.

Of course, this is merely a suggestion and it is probable that the proposer will have other things to say and other points to make but he must make his speech with one eye on the clock – and the faces of his guests. The newly-weds may have a plane to catch and guests are easily bored by a lengthy speech.

The bridegroom
The bridegroom then replies on behalf of his wife and himself, thanking the gathering for their good wishes and gifts; their parents for being their parents and all those who have helped to make the wedding ceremony and the reception a success – concluding with the bridesmaids, and in so doing proposes a toast to 'The bridesmaids'.

In the first part, responding to the toast proposed by the bride's father (or whoever has made it), the bridegroom might refer to:

1. The kindness of his parents during his boyhood, their care and attention to his upbringing.
2. The thanks he owes them for his start in life – and for any particular sacrifices they have made on his behalf.
3. A tribute to his wife's parents and anything they may have provided for the couple's future.
4. Perhaps a short episode of his meeting with his bride, of their engagement, difficulties or fortunes.
5. His intention to devote himself to the happiness of his bride.
    At this point the bridegroom may turn his attention to lighter matters and his toast to the bridesmaids, with perhaps:
6. Thanks to his best man for his assistance and possible nuisance value.
7. A reference to the beauty of the bridesmaids and his thanks for their help during the service.

It is common practice for the bridegroom to present each of the bridesmaids with a small present during his speech (or the bride may do this before the wedding). These presents are by no means mandatory and where given they usually comprise some small piece of jewellery, such as a silver chain with a pendant or a locket or a pair of ear-rings. If there are any pages, they should not be overlooked – some sort of toy is generally most suitable for them.

The best man
The best man then responds on behalf of the bridesmaids. His speech should be light and, as far as possible, filled with humour. From this point there should be no return to emotional references or serious topics – and the ability to make such a speech is often taken very much into consideration by the bridegroom when choosing his best man. He might refer to:

1. The bridegroom's luck in getting the bride he has – and how many another man has wept over her poor choice.
2. The difficulty in getting a scared bridegroom to the altar.
3. The joy he and his friends feel at getting rid of him from their bachelor ranks and their pity for an unfortunate bride.
4. And, of course, the thanks of the bridesmaids for the presents and good wishes they have received from the bridegroom.

(The female best man must be even more tactful than a male best man. If she is a friend of the groom, not a relative, she must avoid giving the impression that she ever wanted to take the bride's place. She may refer – briefly – to her unusual role, perhaps using it as an introduction to an anecdote about the groom's idiosyncrasies. Otherwise the usual guidelines for a best man still apply.)

Other speeches
Those three speeches compose the traditional toasts and replies customary at a wedding reception. No further speeches need be given and, as often as not, they are considered sufficient – but it is by no means uncommon, where time permits, for other guests to speak. One most frequently favoured is a speech of thanks to the host and hostess, given usually by some relative of the bridegroom – followed by a reply from the bride's father, very briefly if he has already spoken.

Other speeches are permissible though the greatest need is to avoid boredom, particularly by insincere guests who like the sound of their own voices or who cannot bear not to have taken some noteworthy part in the proceedings.

With one eye on the time, the best man brings the speeches to an end by rising to read the messages of congratulations and good wishes that have arrived for the newly-weds. In reading them he should endeavour to introduce a few light, background comments on the contents and about those who have sent them. The reading of a large number of telemessages can soon become boring as they are usually repetitions and many of the names will be known to few of the guests.

The best man should remember to hand the telemessages to the bride's mother immediately after the reception to be kept until the bride's return from her honeymoon. It is her duty to write and acknowledge them as soon as possible afterwards – generally at the same time as she writes her thanks to those who have sent presents.

The Cake
The ceremony of cutting the cake either follows the speeches or takes place before them to allow the caterers to remove it and slice it, ready for handing round with the coffee. The bride should place the point of the knife near the centre of the bottom tier of the cake. The bridegroom places a hand over his wife's and slowly and carefully helps her to force the point of the blade down into the heart of the cake and then to draw the blade forwards and downwards. They may cut a complete slice and share it between them, but due to the elaborate decorations on many cakes, the inexperience of the couple, and the probable nervousness of the bride, they rarely make more than a token cut.

Usually that completes the formal 'cutting' of the cake. The caterer takes over from that point and, after dismantling the tiers and ornaments, uses his experience to divide up a tier or two of the cake into handy, not over-large portions which the brides-maids can help to distribute amongst the guests. If there is a large number of guests, the catering staff will do the distribution.

The remainder of the cake will be set aside for eventual distribution to friends and relatives of the newly-weds who have been unable to attend the wedding and the reception afterwards.

It is traditional for the bridesmaids to keep their slices of cake and to place them under their pillows that night – in the belief that they will then dream of their own future husbands.

An Evening Reception

If an evening reception is planned there is often a lull between the wedding breakfast and the arrival of the extra guests in the evening. The hotel or caterers will need to clear the tables from the centre of the room and rearrange them around the edges unless a completely separate room is available for the evening reception. Some guests who have been at the wedding celebrations all afternoon may choose to leave before the evening party gets underway and the bridal couple should be sure to make themselves available to say goodbye to their guests as they leave. Other guests who live close to the reception may take the opportunity to go home for a short while, perhaps to change for the evening.

As the evening guests arrive they will wish to give their congratulations to the newly-weds and to see the bride in her finery. They may well arrive with presents which will need to be stored safely out of harm's way and will want the chance to see any gifts which have already been unwrapped and put on display (see page 90).

Entertainment for the evening usually takes the form of a live band or disco and it is usual for the newly-weds to launch the proceedings with the first dance. An impressive sight can be caused by a couple who have gone to ballroom dance classes in the weeks or months before their wedding to learn steps with which they can sweep across the floor – to the amazement and delight of both friends and family – although the band or disc jockey will need to be warned in advance if a specific piece of music will be wanted. Alternatively, a slow dance could be chosen and other guests could be encouraged to join in as soon as possible if either of the bridal couple are not happy to be the focus of attention on the dance floor. However, it is unlikely that the tradition of the first dance can be avoided altogether!

Food will have to be provided for the evening and the caterer or hotelier will be able to advise on a suitable menu. This usually takes the form of a self-service buffet and is much more informal than the wedding breakfast, with people helping themselves as and when they wish and sitting wherever they choose to eat. If there is still a tier of the wedding cake which has not been cut this could also be displayed on the buffet table and slices can be provided with coffee for those guests who were not at the wedding breakfast if there is enough to go around.

The Departure

Towards the end of the reception the bride retires to change from her wedding finery into her going-away clothes. As she mounts the stairs to the room set aside for this purpose, it is traditional for the bridesmaids to gather at the foot or below the banisters – while the rest of the wedding party stands by to watch the fun.

From a convenient place on the stairs, the bride throws her bouquet to the young ladies gathered below – and the bridesmaid who catches the bouquet can, reputedly, expect to be the next bride. Or she throws her bouquet as she gets into the car to drive away, in a shower of confetti.

While she changes, her baggage is put with the bridegroom's at the exit, all ready to load into the car or taxi that is to take the pair of them on the first stage of their honeymoon.

The bridegroom, if he lives near the venue of the reception (or if one of his friends lives nearby) hurries off with his best man to change into his own going-away clothes. If this is not possible, the bridegroom usually finds a convenient spot among the reception rooms – and as his own dressing should take very much less time than that of his wife, he should be all ready and waiting when she comes down the stairs.

While he is waiting, the bridegroom collects from his best man the rail or air tickets and any other travel documents that he needs for the honeymoon.

(It is often at this time that the young friends of the bridal couple sneak out to 'decorate' the going away car with tin cans, balloons and streamers. Whilst this is considered an essential part of the celebrations by many, it should not be allowed to get out of hand and no damage should be caused to the car.)

When the bride is ready, no further time should be wasted in which emotional scenes may arise. In the years long gone by, partings of this nature were a much more final farewell than they are today. A bride's departure with her husband might have meant a separation for years between her and her parents – sometimes, if they were going abroad, perhaps for ever. Tears and sorrow were natural under such circumstances but modern travel has put the distant parts of the world within a few short hours of home and, with our present standards of living, it is not likely to be impossible for a young couple to save enough for a visit to their parents once in a while. The occasion should therefore be joyful and a mother's inevitable tears kept from sight.

The farewells should be brisk, cheery and smiling. A new and growing custom is for the groom to present his mother and mother-in-law with bouquets of flowers as they say goodbye (although some couples prefer to do this during the groom's speech).

Only after the newly-weds have finally departed for their honeymoon should the guests begin to leave – saying their final goodbyes to the host and hostess (usually the bride's mother and father). Eventually only the hosts and the best man remain behind to clear up the paraphernalia of presents, clothes, wedding cake – and the odds and ends that will surely be forgotten by their owners.

18

AFTER THE SHOW

Before leaving the reception rooms the bride's mother should remember to pick up what is left of the wedding cake. Almost certainly the caterer will have packed it in a box strong enough to protect what is left of the sugary confection.

She must also gather up, pack and take away with her the wedding clothes left behind by her daughter – and make certain that none of her lady guests has left anything behind.

At the same time, someone – often the best man – will pack and take away the discarded clothes of the bridegroom and make sure that arrangements have been made for returning any morning suits or other wedding outfits hired by the groom and best man (and perhaps those of the fathers and the ushers if they all came from the same shop). Also, the best man should see to it that nothing has been left behind by any of the male guests and pass to the bride's mother any greetings messages not already handed to the bride.

If the wedding presents have not been unwrapped during the reception these can probably be transported to the bride's mother's home by the bride's family (perhaps with the help of the best man) immediately at the end of the reception. However, if they have been unwrapped and put on display it may be easier to leave them for a few hours or overnight (as long as they will be safely locked away) until someone such as the best man and some helpers can return with boxes, packing cases, paper and string to re-pack the gifts and transport them safely. They can then be displayed at the home of the bride's parents in some little-used room until they are taken to the home of the newly-weds (see page 91).

The bride's mother will settle down to the task of dividing up sufficient of the wedding cake to be able to send a piece to each of the friends and relatives of the bride and bridegroom who were unable to attend the wedding and the reception afterwards – perhaps because of age, infirmity, illness or distance.

The stationers from whom the wedding invitation cards were obtained may provide the tiny boxes in which to pack the segments of cake. A nice touch would be to have cards printed, fitting the boxes, ready to accompany each piece of cake. The wording will probably be as follows, remembering that the address of the sender will be that of the young couple's new home:

Mr & Mrs Peter J Smith
The Bungalow
Esher Meade

With compliments on the occasion of their wedding.

[Date]

The bride's maiden name could be printed at the top left and crossed through by a silver arrow – and, indeed, all the printing on the card could be in embossed silver. However, this will add extra expense to an already costly occasion and a simpler arrangement is to use standard pre-printed cards that often come with the boxes.

No acknowledgement of the receipt of the cake should be expected.

On the same day the bride's mother and father can send an announcement of the wedding to the press, for publication in the 'Marriages' section of the classified advertisement columns (see Chapter 11). The local paper is the ideal medium if both the bride and bridegroom come from the same district; the local paper should be used in each district when the couple come from different parts of the country – and if it should happen that one or other of them was widely known or famous, then publication should be made in one of the national daily newspapers.

The bride's parents are expected to make the announcement – not those of the bridegroom. This should be remembered in the case where the bridegroom lived in a different town from that of his bride. It is still her mother's duty to send the announcement to the paper in that town though it is quite usual for the bridegroom's mother to undertake the task, by mutual agreement.

The bride's father must settle down to the task of paying the bills that will flow in to him. He used to be responsible for the cost of the reception, including everything to do with it: the cake, the bridal gown and the bridesmaids' attire, the meal, the wines, the cars, the flowers – while the bridegroom, or his father, needed to square the much smaller account for the wedding ceremony. Nowadays, many families share the cost more evenly.

A day or so before the newly-weds are due back from their honeymoon, the bride's parents should take all the wedding presents to their daughter's home.

As soon as they return, the bride is expected to start on the task of writing to thank all those who gave her and her husband wedding presents, and to acknowledge the greetings messages. Letters of thanks need to be handwritten; they should neither be printed nor typed, however burdensome the duty.

Finally, the last act of the wedding ceremony and ritual takes place spread over the next three months. It is the newly-weds' duty to entertain their relatives and friends in their new home – a few at a time, of course, unless the new home is a very large one. Both sets of parents should be invited first, after which priority should go to the best man, the bridesmaids and the ushers (though with them, if there is room in the house, other guests may be added). Then comes the general run of relatives and friends and their entertainment should be settled as a matter of convenience and preference by the bride and bridegroom. The problem is the question of the numbers to be invited on each occasion and whether the invitation is to tea, to a cheese and wine party or to dinner.

No mandatory method applies. The couple are at liberty to please themselves – so long as the entertainment is to be in their own house and not outside. On the face of it, maiden aunts will prefer an invitation to tea, the friends and relatives of the same generation as the newly-weds to a cheese and wine party, and the parents and grandparents perhaps to dinner.

No formal, printed invitations need be sent out. Verbal arrangements or perhaps a brief note would be sufficient – and acceptances will be returned in the same manner.

19

CHOICE OF MENU FOR THE RECEPTION – AT HOME OR AWAY

Likes and dislikes are so individual where food and drink are concerned that it is only possible to make a few tentative suggestions within the scope of a book of this nature. A glance at the cookery shelves in any bookshop or library shows that the scope is unlimited.

The most important point to consider before deciding on a menu is where the meal is to be cooked and served. However expert the amateur cook, it is highly unlikely that home cooking facilities would match that of a first class restaurant or hotel. Even if the bride's mother has in mind a menu that can easily be dealt with in her own kitchen, she needs to be highly organised to undertake the cooking and serving of such a meal since, as hostess, she should normally never have to leave her guests.

However, it is possible to serve a cold meal which can be prepared in advance, plated and ready to serve from a service table or sideboard. For instance, if the bride's mother wanted to give a finger buffet she could serve any of the following:

Vol-au-vents
Sausage rolls
Curry puffs
Individual quiches

which need to be popped into the oven for ten minutes or so to warm through; plus the following served cold:

Fried chicken drumsticks
Cheese and pineapple on cocktail sticks

  Sausages on sticks
  Thin strips of fried fish served with a dip
  Asparagus rolls
  Small sandwiches
  Profiteroles filled with cream cheese
  Small cakes
  Choux buns
  Biscuits

On the other hand, if she felt she could cater for a fork buffet with
three courses, she might start with:

  Savoury mousse or
  Pâté or
  Stuffed eggs

followed by:

  A whole salmon
  Chicken or turkey pieces served in a sauce
  Cold sliced ham, tongue, beef or turkey served with salads
     such as:

  Potato salad
  Mixed bean salad
  Brown rice with corn salad
  Celery, walnut and apple salad

and many others which can be found in any good cookery book.
'Salad' no longer has to mean a lettuce leaf and half a tomato! (It
should be remembered that a number of the guests may be
vegetarian and therefore plenty of interesting meatless dishes
should be included in the menu.)

  Fruit salad with cream and meringues
  Gateaux
  Pavlovas
  Eclairs or choux buns

Trifle with cream

followed by tea or coffee.

If the bride's family have called in a caterer they will be offered a choice of menus to fit their purse. A hot meal is only advisable where there are adequate kitchen facilities or the caterer does not have a long journey. The following are typical of the choice available:

No 1
    Assorted sandwiches
    Filled bridge rolls
    Chicken and mushroom vol-au-vents
    Vegetarian vol-au-vents
    Sausage rolls
    Genoese fancies
    Fruit salad and fresh cream
    Coffee

No 2 (fork buffet)
    Cold ham and tongue
    Veal, ham and egg pie
    Vegetarian quiche
    Potato salad
    Russian salad
    Green salad
    Tomato salad
    Rolls and butter
    Sausage rolls
    Cocktail sausages
    Assorted pastries
    Fruit salad and fresh cream
    Coffee

No 3 (sit down meal)
    Soup or
    Orange and grapefruit cocktail

Rolls and butter
Fillet of Sole Princess
Hot roast chicken with bacon
Mushroom Stroganoff
Buttered new potatoes
Garden peas
Fruit salad and cream
Coffee
Petit fours

No 4 (sit down meal)
Melon cocktail
Smoked salmon with lemon and brown bread
Cold roast turkey with ham
Vegetarian flans
A variety of salads
Croquette or buttered potatoes

Alternatively:
Hot roast turkey with stuffing
Vegetable pilau
Buttered or croquette potatoes
Garden peas

Sherry trifle with cream
Cheese board
Petit fours
Coffee

No 5 (fork buffet)
Lobster or crab mayonnaise
Roast fillet of beef with horseradish sauce
Chicken in cream sauce with pineapple
Stuffed peppers (vegetarian)
Served with green salad and pasta salad
French bread and butter
Lemon soufflé or chocolate gateau
Coffee

No 6 (sit down meal for a summer wedding)
    Melon balls or salmon mousse
    Roast lamb with mint sauce
    Vegetarian stir fry with tofu
    Served with hot new potatoes, green salad, kidney beans,
       carrots, fennel, and chicory in herb vinaigrette salad
    Strawberries or raspberries and cream
    Coffee

If the reception is to be held at a restaurant or hotel, any menu is possible provided the items are available and the hostess is prepared to pay for the meal she envisages. Certainly, hot meals are better in a restaurant or hotel where they have all the facilities on hand and the food can be cooked when required, not hours beforehand then kept warm or re-heated as can happen in a hired hall.

It is usual to offer guests a glass of sherry, white wine or champagne on their arrival at the reception. Increasingly popular is the use of sparkling wines throughout the reception or a still white wine with a good champagne being used for the toasts. As there are often children at weddings as well as those guests who cannot (or do not wish to) drink anything alcoholic, there should always be a good supply of fresh fruit juice, apple and grape juice available and mineral water or perhaps a jug of non-alcoholic fruit punch on each table.

The amount required can be estimated on the basis of six glasses of wine or champagne to each bottle, and the average guest having three to four glasses (or half a bottle of wine) each.

If the reception is to be at home or in a hall, the local wine shop or off-licence can advise on wines and will usually arrange supplies on a sale or return basis. They will often also lend glasses. In a hotel or restaurant, the manager will suggest which wines he has in his cellar and which are the most suitable. They will normally charge for the bottles actually opened.

Many people who are hosting the reception at home or in a hired hall take the opportunity now available to go abroad and get the wine (and perhaps beers) at duty free prices. This can work out cheaper for the alcohol but against this has to be balanced the cost of getting there, transporting the purchases home, and all the extra work involved. Even where this has been done it might still be worth getting some wine from the local off-licence on a sale or return basis to make sure that there is no danger of running out!

Champagnes, white wines and sherries should be chilled – two or three hours in cold water will help where no ice or other coolant is available. Red wines should be served at room temperature by being left on the dining room sideboard for an hour or more before they are to be served. Bottles of red wine should be uncorked about an hour before being served to allow the contents to 'breathe'.

If more than one wine is to be served, remember that dry white wines should be drunk before both red wines and sweet wines, and that younger wines should always be served before older ones.

20

SILVER AND GOLDEN
WEDDINGS

Wedding anniversaries have always been regarded as a purely
private occasion between a man and his wife – except on the rare
days when the 'silver' or 'golden' weddings come around. Other
than those, the anniversaries are usually celebrated with a private
party *à deux*, in whichever way the couple choose: a day out, a
meal in a restaurant followed by a visit to the theatre, or perhaps
a dinner dance or trip to a night club, and often an eternity ring to
mark the first anniversary.

As the years go by, the couple tend to gather about themselves
a family and the regular celebrations tend to become a thing of
the past. Forgotten perhaps; often made impracticable by the
demands of babies. Even then many couples try and mark the day
in at least some way: an exchange of small presents and perhaps
something special for dinner, including a bottle of wine, or
perhaps a meal out.

The years slide past and the couple begin to become so
absorbed in a welter of such events as children's birthdays,
Christmas Days, the school holidays and, in time, their
children's own wedding days, that suddenly – almost unbeliev-
ably – they find the day approaching when they have completed a quarter of a century of married life. Their Silver
Wedding Day.

Something special is called for. First, an announcement in the
press, sent by the couple themselves, might read:

SMITH-JONES – on 20 April [date] at St George's Parish
Church, Woodhouse, Peter John Smith to Ann Jones.
Present address: The Bungalow, Esher Meade.

Secondly, they will exchange gifts and may expect to receive presents from their family and close friends. Where possible, the presents should consist of silver articles, or where this is not feasible because of cost – particularly in the case of gifts from children and grandchildren – the gift should be tied into a parcel with silver ribbon (or using silver paper).

The couple may decide to entertain their children, close friends and, wherever possible, the long ago best man and chief bridesmaid at a small party. Formal invitations are not necessary, but they should be issued well in advance so that those who are to be invited may be given time to make their own arrangements.

Formal wear is not usual except in families where it is customary to attend and dress for functions. The venue can be a hotel or a restaurant and is generally arranged in advance so that a small private room may be reserved for the occasion, or (more often) it is held at home.

A wedding cake usually graces the occasion and, following the meal, it is cut in the same token fashion as applied on the occasion of the wedding itself, twenty-five years earlier.

Speeches are usually few and happy. The eldest son might propose the 'Health and Happiness' of his parents and the husband should reply on behalf of his wife and himself. Other speeches may follow – almost entirely composed of reminiscences – from the best man or one of the guests who was present at the wedding.

The party may move on to a theatre or a dance.

Another quarter of a century may go by and then comes the grand occasion of the Golden Wedding. This time the small party to celebrate the event is usually organised by the eldest son of the couple – often in consultation with his brothers and sisters. He will make the announcement public through the press, in similar fashion to that published twenty-five years before.

On this occasion the presents should be of gold, though very often they are much less valuable and merely tied up with gold coloured ribbon, or wrapped in gold coloured paper.

Again, the party can be held at a hotel or restaurant if at all possible and equally, if possible, the guests of twenty-five years previously should be invited once again – together with the rising generation of grandchildren. Often one of the daughters may arrange the party, do the catering, and hold it in her home.

No formal dress is required, nor need any official invitations be sent out. A cake is usual, though not obligatory.

After the cutting of the cake there may be a few informal speeches but the husband is not compelled to reply in person. Sometimes one of the young grandchildren present performs this office for him – though there is no set order of precedence involved. It is unusual for any sort of entertainment to follow.

At the end of the party it is customary for the eldest son and his wife to escort his parents home. They do not stay when they arrive and none of the guests should follow.

The Diamond Wedding follows on the sixtieth anniversary of their wedding day and follows very much the same lines as the celebrations for the Golden Wedding. However, the presents almost never consist of diamonds and rarely of anything of more intrinsic value than flowers.

The family party should be kept as small as possible and, because of the age of the couple, is usually held either in their own home, or that of one of their children.

The wedding cake need only be a token and, as on previous anniversaries, there is no need for pieces of it to be distributed to absent friends and relatives.

The whole celebration must be geared to the ability of the couple to stand up to the fuss – and, again, the eldest son and his wife should bring the proceedings to a close as soon as tiredness begins to dull the pleasure of the couple.

As a matter of interest, though of little moment today, anniversaries of a wedding are traditionally known as:

1st anniversary ....Paper
2nd anniversary ....Cotton
3rd anniversary ....Leather
4th anniversary ....Silk
5th anniversary ....Wood
6th anniversary ....Iron
7th anniversary ....Wool
8th anniversary ....Bronze

9th anniversary ....Pottery
10th anniversary ....Tin
12th anniversary ....Linen
15th anniversary ....Crystal
20th anniversary ....China
25th anniversary...SILVER
30th anniversary ....Pearl or Ivory
35th anniversary...Coral
40th anniversary ....Ruby
45th anniversary ....Sapphire
50th anniversary...GOLD
55th anniversary ....Emerald
60th anniversary ....DIAMOND
75th anniversary................................and again, DIAMOND

APPENDIX

Some useful addresses
Council of Churches of Britain and Ireland (CCBI), Inter-Church
House, 35-41 Lower Marsh, Waterloo, London, SE1 7RL.
Tel: 0207 620 4444.

Church of England:
The Faculty Office, 1 The Sanctuary, Westminster, London,
SW1P 3JT.
Tel: 0207 222 5881.

Enquiry Centre, Church House, Great Smith Street, London,
SW1P 3NZ.
Tel: 0207 222 9011.

Roman Catholic Church:
Marriage Care, Clitherow House, 1 Blythe Mews, Blythe Road,
London, W14 0NW.
Tel: 0207 371 1341.

Free Churches:
Free Church Federal Council (FCFC), 27 Tavistock Square,
London, WC1H 9HH.
Tel: 0207 387 8413.

Baptist Union, Baptist House, 129 Broadway, Didcot, OX11 8RT.
Tel: 01235 512077.

Methodist Church Office, 25 Marylebone Road, London, NW1 5JR.
Tel: 0207 486 5502.

The United Reformed Church, 86 Tavistock Place, London, WC1H 9RT.
Tel: 0207 916 2020.

Quakers:
Religious Society of Friends, Friends House, 173-177 Euston Road, London, NW1 2BJ.
Tel: 0207 387 3601.

Jewish religion:
Jewish Marriage Council, 23 Ravenshurst Avenue, London, NW4 4EL.

Marriage Authorisation Office, 735 High Road, London, N12 0US.
Tel: 0208 343 6301.
(Office hours: Sunday-Thursday, 10:30am-12:30pm)

General Register Offices:
General Register Office, Smedley Hydro, Trafalgar Road, Birkdale, Southport, PR8 2HH.
Tel: 01704 569824.

General Register Office for Scotland, New Register House, Edinburgh, EH1 3YT.
Tel: 0131 334 0380.

General Register Office, 49-55 Chichester Street, Belfast, BT1 4HL.
Tel: 01232 235211.

Marriage preparation courses:
Lord Chancellor's Department, Family Policy Division, Selbourne House, 54-60 Victoria Street, London, SW1E 6QW. Tel: 0207 210 8718.

Prepare/Enrich Network, Quel Bec, Cothelstone, Taunton, TA4 3ED. Tel: 0800 900099.

INDEX

RIGHT WAY
PUBLISHING POLICY

HOW WE SELECT TITLES

RIGHT WAY consider carefully every deserving manuscript. Where an author is an authority on his subject but an inexperienced writer, we provide first-class editorial help. The standards we set make sure that every **RIGHT WAY** book is practical, easy to understand, concise, informative and delightful to read. Our specialist artists are skilled at creating simple illustrations which augment the text wherever necessary.

CONSISTENT QUALITY

At every reprint our books are updated where appropriate, giving our authors the opportunity to include new information.

FAST DELIVERY

We sell **RIGHT WAY** books to the best bookshops throughout the world. It may be that your bookseller has run out of stock of a particular title. If so, he can order more from us at any time – we have a fine reputation for ''same day'' despatch, and we supply any order, however small (even a single copy), to any bookseller who has an account with us. We prefer you to buy from your bookseller, as this reminds him of the strong underlying public demand for **RIGHT WAY** books. Readers who live in remote places, or who are house-bound, or whose local bookseller is uncooperative, can order direct from us by post.

FREE

If you would like an up-to-date list of all **RIGHT WAY** titles currently available, please send a stamped self-addressed envelope to ELLIOT RIGHT WAY BOOKS, BRIGHTON ROAD,
LOWER KINGSWOOD, TADWORTH, SURREY, KT20 6TD, U.K.
or visit our web site at www.right-way.co.uk